Golf for Women

Golf for Women

Kathy Whitworth

with

Rhonda Glenn

St. Martin's Press   New York

Design by Karin Batten

Library of Congress Cataloging-in-Publication Data

Whitworth, Kathy.
    Golf for women / Kathy Whitworth & Rhonda Glenn.
        p.   cm.
    ISBN 0-312-04013-X
    1. Golf for women.   I. Glenn, Rhonda.   II. Title.
    GV966.W47 1990
    796352'04042—dc20   89-78002
                                                          CIP

First Edition

10 9 8 7 6 5 4 3 2 1

Contents

Acknowledgments

All of the photographs for Part I of this book were shot by Dost & Evans Golf Graphics. Many thanks for their careful work.

Foreword

I often talk to golfers about what it takes to become a champion. Among the most important qualities are desire, dedication, determination, concentration, and the will to win. Kathy Whitworth has these qualities more than any golfer I know.

Kathy has won eighty-eight official LPGA tournaments, more than any woman or man, in professional golf. One of the qualities that has also made Kathy a great champion is that when she has had a rare bad round, she analyzes it. When she goes to her hotel room at night, she thinks about her game and her swing. She thinks, ''Where did I go wrong here? What can I do to improve tomorrow?'' In this way, she has become a great student of the game.

Kathy has been winning on the LPGA Tour for thirty years. During that time, she has really studied the game. In this book, she passes on her knowledge to you. If you study her book, you will have a better understanding of what it takes to play good golf, or even great golf.

Kathy Whitworth, I am proud to say, is also a great friend of mine and I'm honored that she asked me to write the foreword to *Golf for Women*.

—PATTY BERG
Fort Myers, Florida
December, 1989

Preface

There are no absolutes in golf. Golf is such an individual game, and no two people swing alike. Even the best golfers have their own swings and their own way of getting into the proper positions.

For that reason, until now I've been reluctant to write a book of golf instruction because I believe that the best lessons are learned on the practice tee with a good teaching professional.

However, in my thirty-five years of golf, I've learned *why* certain things must happen in the golf swing. If I had to single out one factor that has helped me win tournaments over the years, it is this understanding of the why's of golf. Golf became much easier for me when I began to understand why the club has to come into the ball in a certain way, why the grip has to be a certain way, and so forth.

In trying to conquer this game—and by no means have I conquered golf, no one ever does—I've constantly pondered why a technique can't work another way. Gradually, I began to figure it out. I also had a lot of help from a wonderful teacher, Harvey Penick, of Austin, Texas, who helped me understand the why's: why the club should do certain things and follow certain patterns.

It's true that golfers have their own way of getting to the proper positions. They can even play fairly well if they do it in an unorthodox way, but it makes the game so much more difficult.

For example, if you come into the ball with a closed clubface instead of a square clubface, you must be *extremely* strong in the left side to avoid duck-hooking the ball. Some golfers make that adjustment and do quite well, but it would be much simpler if the clubface were square. They wouldn't have to make adjustments. The fewer adjustments you make in your swing, the better off you are.

I'm not writing or showing anything in this book that hasn't been said before or that hasn't been emphasized through other people's teachings. It's just that I might be able to give you a different slant on golf's principles and help you to better understand the swing and the game.

—KATHY WHITWORTH
Roanoke, Texas, 1989

PART I

The Fundamentals
of Golf

The Fundamentals of the Golf Swing

I really believe that women need to work on the fundamentals of the golf swing. Because women are not as strong as men, it's even more important for them to be fundamentally correct in form than it is for men.

These are the fundamentals of the golf swing: grip, stance, clubface alignment, ball position, weight distribution, and the position of the hands at address. It's very difficult for a player to have a good golf swing without good fundamentals. The swing happens in steps, in a sequence. For example, if you have a bad grip, you can't take the club back properly, nor can you make a proper weight shift. These fundamentals are the mechanics to achieve a *swing* that involves good timing, rhythm, and balance.

I firmly believe that there are no absolutes in this game. There are many types of golf swings and many players who don't follow the principles I favor. I'm not saying that they can't play that way, I'm just saying that to have a consistent golf swing, it's better to do it this way. If you can make your golf swing simple and use techniques that have been proven over the years, it will be much easier to build a repetitively good golf swing.

Some players have little quirks in their swings. I have one in mine—a loop. When I take the club away from the ball, I take the club back on the outside and drop to the inside. I'm not advocating that you have such a loop, because it's harder to time. I would dearly like to get out of that loop, but it is mine, and I can be effective with it. Despite this quirk, I'm able to get in good position in the impact area. If you can get the club into position through that vital hitting area—about one foot before you contact the ball, at impact, and about one foot after contact—then you too can be effective. How you get there is really up to you. This book contains

3

thoughts that can help you achieve that good swing. They are not absolutes and they are not printed in stone. It is untrue that if you don't do these things you cannot be a great player. Many great players don't have perfect golf swings, but all great players do certain things alike. Most good teachers will show you pictures of good players, point out certain positions in their swings, and explain that these are the positions you must attain somehow if you are to have a good swing. I'm going to tell you how *best* to get there, but that doesn't mean that you can't get there another way.

THE GRIP

The hands are your only contact with the club. That's why the grip is so important. There are three types of grips: the interlocking grip, the overlapping grip, and the baseball grip. The same principle applies to all grips: The hands must fit together in order to work together in the swing. If the hands are separated on the club, they

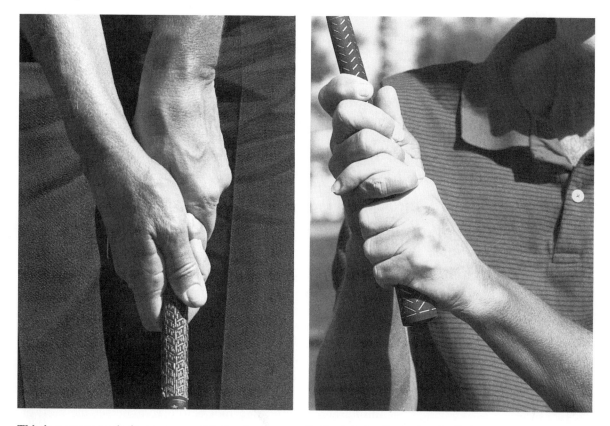

This is a correct grip in every way. My hands are on the club securely and the Vs are closed.

In the interlocking grip, the little finger of the right hand interlocks with the forefinger of the left hand.

tend to fight one another. For example, the right hand of right-handed players might become too dominant instead of bringing the weaker left hand, and most importantly, the left side of the body, into play. A good grip unites both hands on the club. In taking the grip, I think it's important to have equal pressure in both hands.

This pressure should not create tension in the forearms. You need the flexibility in your arms so that they can swing the club with control and speed. Too much tension in the hands and arms restricts them from getting in position to hit the ball with power.

The interlocking grip involves interlocking the little finger of the right hand between the index finger and the middle finger of the left hand. These two fingers entwine with each other. Jack Nicklaus uses this grip with great success. The interlocking grip works well because it keeps the hands together, rather than letting the hands separate at some crucial point in the swing. I recommend that women, especially women who have short fingers, consider using an interlocking grip, because it will give you a stronger grip. In the game's

In the overlapping grip, the little finger of the right hand overlaps the forefinger of the left hand.

In the baseball grip, all of the fingers are on the club, with no interlocking and no overlapping.

evolution, the interlocking was probably the first grip. Then the great British golfer Harry Vardon popularized the overlapping grip, which is sometimes called the Vardon grip.

In the overlapping grip, the little finger of the right hand overlaps the index finger and middle finger of the left hand.

In the baseball grip, all the fingers are on the club with no interlocking and no overlapping. One fine player on our tour, Beth Daniel, uses the baseball grip and is very successful with it.

I used the interlocking grip when I began playing golf as a youngster because my hands were small. My hands later became larger and, as time went on, it seemed better for me to use an overlapping grip.

When we look at pictures of a good player taking a grip, we immediately have a problem. Most pictures show the left hand, palm up, with the club lying across the palm and fingers. This is misleading. It implies that a player comes at the grip from the bottom. Actually, you should take your grip by putting your hands down on the club **from the top**.

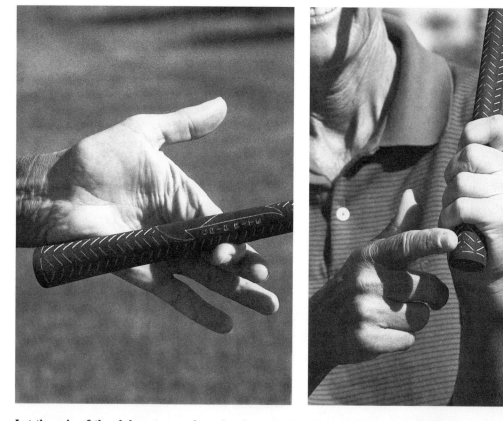

Let the grip of the club rest securely under the pad of the left hand. This will give you more support at the top of the swing.

The end of the club should extend about ¼ inch beyond the heel of the left hand.

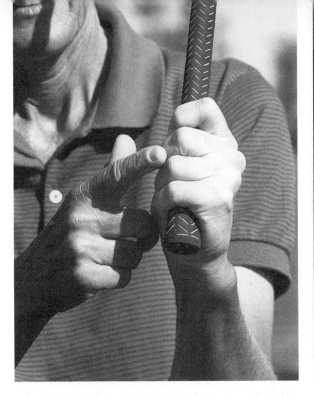

The main pressure points of the left hand are in the last three fingers.

My left hand is on the club correctly. The club is in the palm and fingers of the left hand.

Here, my left hand is on the club correctly, and the blade of the club is square.

This is incorrect. The blade is open.   **This is also incorrect. The blade is closed.**

Lower the left hand onto the club so that the grip of the club is diagonal across your palm and fingers. The grip of the club lies under the heel of the left hand. Then close the left hand naturally. It's very difficult to understand a proper grip without seeing it, so please study the photographs of my grip on page 4.

If the club is held completely in the palm of the left hand, it will create a gap between the left thumb and the left forefinger. If held only in the fingers, it would be very hard to close that gap. The gap between the thumb and forefinger is called the V. I believe this V must be closed by putting the thumb and forefinger snugly together.

If you close this V, the natural position of the thumb will be on top of the grip of the club. This correct thumb position will help you control the club at the top of the backswing. At the top of the swing, the club shaft should actually rest on that thumb. This will help keep you from overswinging or losing the grip at the top of the swing.

A closed V also enables you to put your right hand on the club properly. The right hand should fit snugly against the left hand so that both hands can work together in the swing.

The point of the Vs of both hands should point to an imaginary spot somewhere between the chin and the right shoulder. Because we are all made differently, and our joints are different, we can have some variation, but the Vs should point in that general direction.

8

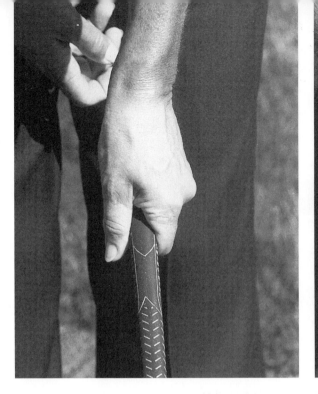

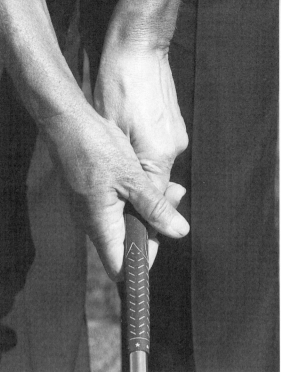

This is the wrong way to do it! The V formed by the thumb and forefinger of the left hand is open, when it should be closed.

This is also incorrect. The V formed by the thumb and forefinger of the right hand is also open. It should be closed.

If your hands are too much underneath the shaft when you take your grip, your grip is referred to as too strong. This means that not only is your left hand too strong, but your right hand is also very strong. This can cause problems. For example, a very strong right hand makes you want to pull the club back at the beginning of your backswing with your right arm and right hand. That's why the left hand is so important. The left hand keeps the right hand, and therefore the right side of the body, from taking over.

If you put your left hand on the club correctly, you can easily put your right hand down on top of the left in correct position. The

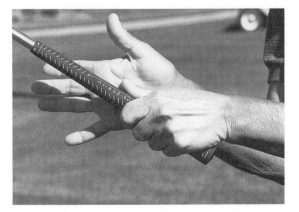

When placing the right hand on the club, the lifeline fits snugly over the left thumb.

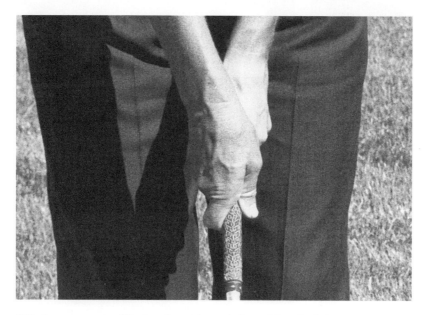

This is a poor grip. The hands are in a weak position, both hands turned too far to the left, and I will probably hit a slice.

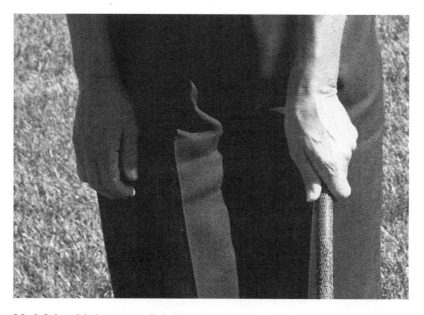

My left hand is incorrect. It is in a strong position, which simply means my hand is turned too far to the right. I would probably hit a hook from this position.

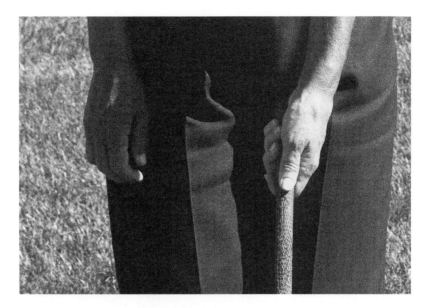

My left hand is incorrect. It is in a weak position, in other words, turned too far to the left, and can create a slice.

If your grip is too strong, both hands turned too far to the right, as in this picture, your right hand will take over on your backswing.

right thumb should rest just to the left side of the clubshaft, not directly on top of the shaft, and the left thumb should similarly rest just on the right side of the shaft.

If this is done correctly, at the top of the backswing both thumbs will be underneath the clubshaft, which gives you more control of the club. The club shaft will actually rest on the thumbs.

This is a good swing clue. If the thumbs aren't under the shaft at the top of the backswing, it is a good indication that your hands are not in the proper position. However, if you think you have a good grip and your thumbs are not under the shaft at the top of the backswing, then you have two possible problems: either the plane, or path, of your swing is too flat or too upright, or your hands are

If you have a good grip, the thumb of the left hand helps support the clubshaft at the top of the swing.

This is incorrect. At the top of the backswing, the left thumb should be under the clubshaft to support the club in a good position.

in a bad position, with the grip either open (positioned too far to the left on the club), or closed (positioned too far to the right on the club). This is a key to use in correcting yourself.

GRIP CHECKLIST

- Study pictures of a good grip.
- Put your hands on the club from the top.
- Lower your left hand onto the club so that the grip lies diagonally across the palm and fingers, with the club below the heel of the hand. Close the hand naturally.
- Close the V between the left thumb and left forefinger.
- Lower the right hand onto the club, snugly against the left, in either an interlocking, overlapping, or baseball grip.
- Make sure the right thumb lies on the left side of the club.
- Close the V between the right thumb and right forefinger.
- Make sure both Vs point to an imaginary spot between the chin and the right shoulder.

ALIGNMENT

Alignment is the relationship of your body's position with the line to the target. It relates to the direction in which you want the ball to travel.

At address, your body doesn't face the target head-on. However, the clubface is facing the target, and the position of your body—feet, hips, and shoulders—is on a line at right angles to the face of the club.

This relative position of your clubface, feet, hips, and shoulders, when you are lined up to the target, is crucial to making a good golf swing. Many times, there's really nothing wrong with your swing other than bad alignment. Once your alignment is corrected, your swing sort of falls into the groove.

Poor alignment can make you develop bad swing habits. For example, it can make you start your downswing with the upper part of your body, which is called "coming over the top." Other poor habits can make you come over the top—not using your legs, or using an incorrect weight shift. There are reasons for an incorrect move in the golf swing, and poor alignment could very easily be one of them. If you are coming over the top, for example, you may be lined up too far to the right. This will make you unconsciously try to pull the shot back to the correct line to the target. If you are fading the ball (hitting it in an exaggerated left-to-right flight path), nine times out of ten you are lined up to the left of the target and are subconsciously trying to push the shot back to the line to the target.

The first thought in developing good alignment is that a square clubface goes hand in hand with the grip. A square clubface is one that is in position to hit the ball in a direct line toward your target. When the clubhead is resting on the ground, you should grip it with

For correct alignment, first set the clubface behind the ball with the blade facing the target.   **Then take your stance, making sure your feet, hips, and shoulders are square to the target.**

Here's a side view of a good, square alignment position.

the blade square. In other words, the face of the club should be facing neither left nor right, but squarely ahead. It's no good to first grip the club, then try to maneuver your hands around to make the clubface square. The face must first be square; *then* you take your grip.

Good alignment actually comes from having a square clubface at address. First, set the blade down behind the ball facing directly down the line of flight. Now it is square. Then, step into your stance. Your body should be square to the clubface. Since the clubface is square to your target, your body is also square to your target.

Once you feel comfortable that the clubface is square, step into your stance with your feet, hips, and shoulders at a 90-degree angle to the clubface. This is a set procedure. You should repeat it each time you take your stance. Repetition builds confidence. You can

This is a hook stance. My right foot is pulled back from the line of flight, which is indicated by the yardstick I've placed on the grass.

In a hook stance, the hips and shoulders are also angled back, instead of square to the target.

consistently look at your target and feel comfortable that you are lined up correctly. You won't be questioning yourself, thinking, "Am I lined up properly?"

My instructor Harvey Penick taught me a good key. Once I've addressed the ball and feel as though I'm lined up correctly, I hold the club in both hands and lay it across my thighs. I just let the club lie there. I don't force it. If the club is pointing a bit to the left or right of my target, I know that I'm lined up a little to the left or right and I can make an adjustment.

Alignment is like a railroad track. Your shoulders and feet point down one rail of the track line and your clubface points down the other rail, which is perpendicular. The line of the clubface points directly at the target, therefore the line of your shoulders, hips, and feet points just a couple of feet to the left of the target.

When you're hitting balls on the practice tee, you can have some-

Here I'm showing an open stance. My shoulders and hips, as well as my feet, are open, lined up to the left of the target.

In an open stance, the left foot is pulled back from the line to the target, which I've indicated by placing a yardstick on the grass.

one check your alignment. You can also check yourself by placing a club on the grass next to the ball. Align the club to where you want the ball to go, then step into your stance and try to be square to that club.

On the golf course, you can do the same thing while waiting for someone else to play, just to check yourself. Of course, you cannot leave a club on the ground to point out your line because that violates the Rules of Golf.

Unfortunately, many women don't practice alignment, although it is one of the areas where practice is most important. Videos of your swing are good too because you can watch the tape to see whether you have a tendency to line up too much to the left or right, and you can check to see that your shoulders, feet, and hips are square to the clubface.

ALIGNMENT CHECKLIST

- As you grip the club, make sure the clubface is square.
- Set the clubface behind the ball, making sure it squarely faces the intended target.
- Step into your stance with your feet, hips, and shoulders at right angles to the clubface.
- Check your alignment frequently in practice.

STANCE

The key to the width of your stance is the width of your shoulders. In taking your stance, the outsides of your feet should be as far apart as the width of your shoulders.

Women should have a little wider stance than men because women have a wider hip base, so they need more solid support. Women might also feel a bit stronger with a wider stance, although you must be careful not to overdo it.

If your stance is too wide, you will restrict your swing. You will not have room to shift your weight and make a turn.

If your stance is too narrow, you become top heavy and the top of your body starts to tilt during the swing. You will have too much movement of your top half, and therefore you have no control.

I always refer to the stance as a bit like a child's playswing; something has to be stationary for a swing to work. Whether it's a child's playswing or a golf swing, there has to be a center of gravity. If the base of the golf swing moves, the swing moves too, and there's no way you can swing a golf club with any force—it *sways* instead of *swings*.

When you take your stance, the width of the outsides of your feet should be about the same as the width of your shoulders.

STANCE CHECKLIST

- Make sure the outsides of your feet are as far apart as the width of your shoulders.
- An overly wide stance restricts your swing.
- An overly narrow stance causes a body tilt in the swing.

WEIGHT DISTRIBUTION

At address, the weight should be evenly distributed on both feet, from the ball of the foot to the heel. This gives you a more solid base. You are starting equally, unless you are trying to play a specialty shot, which we'll get into later.

At address, keep the back fairly straight but don't stand up like a stick. I've heard different phrases: Pretend you're sitting down on a stool, or brace yourself as if you're getting ready to receive a punch, as if someone is going to hit you, and flex your knees slightly.

At address, your weight should be on the insides of your feet.

This stance is too upright. It will cause you to change levels throughout the swing. (See photo sequence on pages 34 and 35.)

Too much flex in the knees at address will also cause you to change levels throughout the swing.

Standing too far from the ball throws the weight to the toes.

Standing too close to the ball puts the weight too far back toward the heels.

I am amused sometimes watching players because I can tell that, at some point, someone told them to flex their knees. They address the ball and, just before they take the club back, they squat. That's okay, but you can bend them too much.

Rather than bend from the waist, you should bend over the ball from the hip joint at the top of the thigh. Then flex your knees a little, just to give yourself a little support so that you are in balance. Bending a little from the hip joint will help you determine how far to stand from the ball. You won't have to worry about reaching for the ball or standing too close to it, either of which would throw you out of balance.

At address, as you bend from the hip you should let your arms hang naturally. This will also help you determine the proper distance to stand from the ball.

At address, you should bend slightly from the hip joints, at the top of your legs, as I'm demonstrating here.

If you are the right distance from the ball, with good weight distribution, your arms will be free to swing around your body. You won't feel restricted. This will also enable you to swing, to turn your shoulders and hips, with little restriction. From the proper address position, your arms will be free to swing and your club will be free to swing.

WEIGHT DISTRIBUTION CHECKLIST

• Distribute weight equally on both feet, with weight between the ball of the foot and the heel.
• Keep your back fairly straight, but relaxed.
• Bend over the ball from the top of the thigh.
• Flex your knees slightly.
• Let your arms hang naturally from your body.

In a correct address position, the back is fairly straight, the shoulders are relaxed, and the arms hang naturally. My knees are slightly flexed and I have bent over the ball from the hip joint at the top of the thigh.

BALL POSITION

Ball position is important because each club is a different length.

The shorter the club, from the wedge up to the 7-iron, the closer you play the ball to the center of your stance. There's a reason for that: With a shorter club the bottom of the swing arc is going to fall quicker, at about the center of your stance, than it would with a longer club. So play the ball a little back, or toward the center of your stance, because you want to ensure that you hit the ball first, and the turf afterward.

As you progress into the middle irons, then into the longer irons, the ball is played a little to the left of the center of your stance. It can vary a bit. It doesn't have to be exact.

Play the ball between the heel and instep of the left foot when using your driver. For fairway woods, play the ball just a bit farther back.

When using short irons, play the ball in the center of your stance.

When using medium irons, play the ball just slightly left of the center of your stance.

When using long irons, play the ball left of the center of your stance.

Play your fairway woods about even with the heel of the left foot. You still want to contact the ball on the downward part of your swing arc. If you try to hit the ball on the upswing, you'll lose control. We're still trying to control the ball with the fairway woods. We often use fairway woods to hit to the green, so we have to hit them fairly straight, and control is essential.

You will develop more accuracy with fairway woods by contacting the ball first, then the turf.

It wouldn't work to play the ball off the center of your stance with a driver. The longer the club, the later in the swing is the bottom of the arc. However, the driver should be played no farther left than the instep of the left foot. You want to catch the driver on the upswing.

It's harder to get the driver airborne because it has a deep clubface, which is why we put the ball on a tee. The higher you tee the ball, the more apt you are to hook it or really miss it. Tee it up with about half of the ball above the clubhead. I don't think you need to tee the ball higher than that.

BALL POSITION CHECKLIST

- Wedge through 7-iron: Play the ball close to the center of your stance.
- 6-iron through 2-iron: Play ball left of the center of your stance.
- Fairway woods and driver: Play the ball off of the left heel.
- When hitting the driver, tee up the ball with about half of the ball above the clubhead.

HAND POSITION AT ADDRESS

The hands should be at least even with the ball, or slightly ahead. If the hands are too far ahead of the ball at address, it can cause a backswing that is too upright.

A good key is that your hands should never be more forward than the center of the left thigh.

Also, do not put your hands *behind* the ball because that would bring the club into the hitting area in a position which would make you hit behind the ball, contacting the turf first, then the ball. Or, you might contact the ball and the turf at the same time. That would create loss of control and loss of distance.

HAND POSITION CHECKLIST

- Always have the hands in a position at least even with the ball, not behind it.
- Position the hands no more forward than the center of the left thigh.

This is a correct hand position. The hands are slightly ahead of the ball, about even with the left thigh.

This position is incorrect. My hands are too far ahead of the ball.

In this picture, I have deliberately put my hands too far behind the ball. This is also incorrect.

Putting it all together: This is a good picture of a correct grip, a square blade, and a square stance.

Using the Left Side

The golfer's left side must be the dominant part of the swing. This is the only way to get the maximum power and accuracy. If the right side takes over, there is no golf swing.

This is not to say that you do not use the right side for some power, but the left side cannot collapse. Even on the backswing the left side must be in control; it swings the club.

Some top players minimize the role of the left side, but they may not realize what they are actually *doing* during the swing. Study the golf swing of any top player and you will see that the left side moves through the hitting area first and is the side that controls the clubhead.

I stress fundamentals, or things that must occur in a good golf swing, because they are things I have been taught. Now, after years of playing and competing, I know why these things must happen to maximize a golf swing. Golfers can swing the club many different ways. No two people have identical swings, but, as I've said, they do certain fundamental things the same way.

Some players and teachers today have a theory of hitting from the right side, hitting with the right hand, or feeling that they are pitching the ball with the right side. To some degree, that's okay, but if the left side does not come through the shot and remain strong throughout the swing, this theory will not work because the player has no control of the clubhead.

28

On the backswing, I'm staying level, moving neither up nor down, and there is no lateral movement.

At the top of the backswing, I'm square, with the left arm and left side strong and in control.

On the downswing, my weight shifts back to the left. There's a lateral move with the legs. The left side (left hand and shoulder) still leads throughout the swing.

My hands are moving past my body and my weight continues to move to the left side.

The momentum of a good swing pulls you through to a balanced finish, as shown by these two photographs.

INITIATING YOUR BACKSWING WITH THE LEFT SIDE

In starting the club back, the left hand and the left side of the body swing the club to the top of the backswing. The great teacher Ernest Jones demonstrated this by swinging a string with a rock tied to the end of the string. My teacher Harvey Penick, who has so successfully taught many great players like Ben Crenshaw, Betsy Rawls, and Tom Kite, demonstrated the start of the backswing by saying it's like swinging a bucket of water.

Harvey wanted a one-piece move away from the ball and he would actually demonstrate, with the bucket of water, the forward press to initiate the swing.

You wouldn't swing a bucket of water from a total standstill because that would be a very jerky motion. Harvey showed me that in the backswing as well as in swinging a bucket of water, you move a little forward first, then you move back. That creates a one-piece takeaway. That's why most great players have some type of move to initiate the swing, like a waggle or perhaps a slight press with the right knee. Mickey Wright did that and Patty Berg had a bit of that. Lee Trevino has what golf announcers refer to as his little dance step. That's Lee's forward press and his way of initiating the swing, but each individual player has to develop her own.

30

I was taught these principles by Harvey Penick and Hardy Loud-ermilk at an early age. Since I've become a better player and more of a student of the game, I've discovered why they taught those principles to me.

Each golf student needs to be told, and have it reaffirmed, that the left side must be the dominant side in the swing. That's why a correct grip is so important and why the left hand must be put on the club correctly so that the left side will be strong. If the left side is strong, the right side will pretty much take care of itself. I know that sounds almost too easy, but it's one of the great fundamentals of golf. Also, with a correct grip, the right elbow will fold in almost automatically on the backswing.

ARE YOU USING YOUR LEFT SIDE?

How can you tell if your left side is strong? If it isn't, the right side has taken over and the clubface will come into the ball a few degrees open or closed, rather than square.

If your left hand is on the club properly when you take your grip and if your clubface is square, when you take the club back the left hand and left side are guiding that clubface to remain square on the backswing.

31

If any part of your right side takes over, either going back or coming down, it will change the clubface. This error will also make you stop, and you won't be able to move your weight to your left side with the left side swinging through. You'll hook or slice, depending on the position of the clubface and how much you let the right side take over.

Practice keeping your left side strong throughout your swing and you will have mastered one of the most important keys of the golf swing.

LEFT SIDE CHECKLIST

- Develop a correct grip.
- Use a smooth, one-piece takeaway.
- On the backswing, allow the left hand and left side to guide the clubface and keep it in its square position.
- Through impact and on the follow-through, do not allow the right side to dominate the swing.

Staying Level

One principle that will help any player, I believe, is staying on the same level throughout the swing. You cannot move up and down. Everything—knees, body, head—must stay on the same level.

Many women golfers move their upper bodies up and straighten their knees as they swing. The woman golfer often picks the club up, with her body going up, instead of staying down over the ball, or staying level. Men do that to some degree, but I think it's more prevalent among women.

You cannot swing the golf club unless something is stationary, as in the base of a child's playswing, which I mentioned earlier. If the child's playswing went up and down vertically, it would lose its swing. The same principle applies to the golf swing. Your body must be fairly stationary. If you move up and down, you're not really swinging; you're pulling the club straight up as you move up, then down, as you move down. This creates inconsistency in your swing and in the quality of your golf game. If you stay on the same level, you have a much better chance of coming back close to the position from which you started. Keeping your head on the same level helps eliminate any up-and-down motion.

However, you *can* move laterally a little bit and get away with it because you're not moving up and down. This lateral shift is associated with weight shift, which we will discuss in the next section.

Some of the great players, like Jack Nicklaus, Louise Suggs, and, most recently, Curtis Strange, allow their head to move a little laterally. I think a *slight* lateral move is good because it keeps you from getting too restricted, helps your rhythm, and probably helps create a longer arc on your backswing which, in turn, creates more clubhead speed.

33

The photographs across this spread show what I mean by "changing levels" in the swing. This is incorrect and will cause many problems.

As long as you don't overdo the lateral movement, you can get away with it, but an extreme lateral movement will put you out of position. That's why I advocate swinging your weight to the inside of the right foot on the backswing, and not to the outside. Your weight must stay on the inside of the right foot at the top of the backswing.

You can move the upper part of the body (the head and shoulders) laterally, but the lower part of the body, your base, does not move laterally. The lower part of the body is stationary and simply turns out of the way to the inside of the right foot—that's the feeling for which you should strive.

You will do this automatically if you keep the right knee flexed and you're balanced.

Some teachers advocate shifting your weight to your right heel on the backswing. This is another method to help you make a proper backswing.

STAYING LEVEL CHECKLIST

- Don't ''pick up'' the club, or allow the upper body to go up on the backswing.
- Keep your head level during the swing.

The Legs Must Do the Work

You must try to keep the golf swing as simple as you can. That is why I'm so adamant about fundamentals. You will develop more understanding of the golf swing as you go along.

Often we look at results within the swing, rather than causes. We may say the club is in the wrong position, and break the swing down into pieces, but we don't really think about what caused it. That's why our great golf instructors are so good. They have figured out the causes.

Harry Vardon, the great English player who is commonly credited for developing the modern grip, discovered if he gripped the club a certain way he would perform better. But why? That's the essential question. Vardon discovered that this overlapping grip would help him keep his hands close together at the top of the backswing, and resulted in better clubhead speed at contact. This is a cause and result.

Remember, all we're trying to do is to swing that clubhead with as much control and power as possible, for an end result that is straight and long.

One of the few really revolutionary concepts of the golf swing came from Byron Nelson. He developed the concept of using the legs as the dominant source of power and control in the golf swing. One evening at dinner I was talking with Byron about how he developed that revolutionary theory. Before Byron's work (which he developed, incidentally, to take advantage of the newly introduced steel shafts), most players were strictly "hands" players. The old clubs had hickory shafts that had a lot of flexibility, or play, in them. The hands worked to control that play. Byron and his friend, professional George Jacobus, analyzed Byron's swing,

36

The legs must be flexed at address and on the backswing.

using the new steel shafts, and developed the theory of using the tremendous drive and power of the legs. They truly developed the modern swing. It was terribly interesting to me, hearing firsthand from Byron how that swing evolved from his work with Jacobus on the practice tee.

USING THE LEGS FOR POWER

I've always felt that my legs provide my power. The power for most women comes from their legs because we are not as strong above the waist as men. For most women, the bulk of weight is below the waist.

Many of our longest hitters on the tour, like Pat Bradley, Patty Sheehan, and Debbie Massey, are ex-skiers. Their legs are well developed and provide their power. They're not really large women, nor particularly tall, but they have very strong legs.

The legs should remain flexed throughout the downswing.

To use the legs, they must be flexed. Again, we go back to balance. If you're going to do something with that clubhead, you've got to be ready. Slightly flexed legs at address are called a "ready stance." Your weight is balanced on the balls and heels of the feet, so that you can use your feet!

By shifting your weight and by getting your body into the swing, you will have more power. Therefore, if you want to swing the clubhead faster, you must use your legs and the lower part of your body. Power doesn't come from flailing at the ball as hard as you can. Power comes from using your legs. Using the legs correctly comes from a good weight shift.

Let's go back to the child's playswing. Like the frame of that playswing, our legs and lower body form the frame of our golf swing. The body must remain stationary, and the clubhead, club, and arms swing away from the body. Your weight should shift across the inside of the left foot to the inside of the right foot. Your right knee should remain slightly flexed and act as a brace.

If you have no brace, you cannot push back into the shot to initiate the downswing. Without the brace of the right knee, the only way to initiate the downswing would be to lunge with the top part of the body. That lunge would throw the club out of its path in relation to the target.

If your weight went to the outside of the right foot, or your right knee straightened on the backswing, your body would tend to move upward. It would then be very difficult to have a good hip turn and shoulder turn. You would simply tilt, rather than turn. This is sometimes called "over-swinging."

I believe you must be taught to use your legs. Using your legs, however, is pretty much automatic once you learn the weight shift and the reasons the weight should only shift in a certain way.

I don't lift my left heel off the ground at the top of my backswing, although most teachers advocate it. Lifting the heel slightly gives you a little bigger arc and a greater shoulder turn. The heel doesn't really lift as much as it sort of rolls up. Many golfers do it incorrectly by going up on their left toe. As a young player, I couldn't seem to do it correctly either, so Harvey Penick told me to keep it on the ground. This is a very individual part of my own swing.

I simply try to put the club into a certain position. That's also what Ernest Jones advocated; if you swing the clubhead, the shoulder turn will happen and the hip turn will happen. *They are results*. They are not something that you have to work on. I never worked on a shoulder turn. All I was concerned with was swinging that clubhead and moving that clubhead to the top of the swing in the right position.

USING YOUR LEGS CHECKLIST

- Keep the legs flexed and relaxed at address.
- Develop a good weight shift.
- At the top of the backswing, keep the right knee slightly flexed and the weight on the inside of the right foot.

Tempo: The Forgotten Fundamental

Smooth tempo is another important fundamental of a good golf swing, one that is, unfortunately, sometimes ignored.

Tempo and timing are based on everything working together. Let's go back to the child's playswing. If it gets jerky, it just doesn't swing; if something makes the chain jerk, you don't get a good swing. This is tempo.

When the golfer is at the height of her backswing, as when on a child's playswing, she feels almost as if she comes to a complete stop before she starts down. This isn't really true, of course, but you *almost* come to a stop because there is a hesitation, of sorts, when you change direction.

When you start your downswing, you swoosh down through the ball and then slow your swing automatically at the follow-through. Therefore, your maximum clubhead speed is right down at the bottom of the swing. That's what you're striving for, maximum timing at the bottom of the swing, or at the ball.

It's as if you were swinging that pail of water. If you jerk it back, it throws your tempo and timing off. Tempo and timing are basically the same thing. When instructors tell you that your tempo or timing is off, they are trying to get you to swing with everything working together.

I cannot tell you here to swing slowly or to swing fast. Each player has a different tempo. Some golfers are very deliberate. Nancy Lopez is very deliberate when she takes the club back. It would be disastrous for her if we said, "Okay, Nancy, we're going to speed it up."

If she tried to speed up her swing, it would throw her completely out of sync. Other players, like Lanny Wadkins and Tom Watson, are quite fast. That's just the way they swing and there's nothing wrong with that. We're all geared differently. Some of us are more highly strung, some of us are very low-key. Some people walk slowly, others walk swiftly. That's just inbred.

HOW TO GET IN SYNC

There is one very simple key to help you have a smooth tempo. When I see someone whose timing is a little off, I always tell the person to slow down the first move away from the ball.

This is a procedure I follow in my own golf swing. You can't go from zero to 60 m.p.h. and then expect to accelerate through the ball. So, if you can make that first move away from the ball a very deliberate one, you'll develop smoother tempo.

All of us are trying to get more clubhead speed, but if that first move away from the ball is a fast one, it just won't work. You must give yourself time to create clubhead speed, just as when swinging in a child's playswing. That's also why you really need to develop some sort of forward press, to give yourself that little extra momentum so that when you come back down through the ball you are generating clubhead speed.

You need to be very smooth in the first 12 inches of your backswing. If everyone could do that, myself included, we could correct a lot of mistakes.

Golfers say, "Yesterday I hit the ball just great and today I couldn't hit anything." What they often don't realize is that their swing did not change overnight—their feel and timing changed.

That's why great players like Louise Suggs, Patty Berg, and Jack Nicklaus developed a routine of addressing the ball. If their routine is interrupted in any way, they step away from the ball and start over because they are using that routine to get their tempo and rhythm going.

Jack always said, "I'm not going to swing until I'm ready!" And he doesn't! Good players develop different routines. Jack spotlines his shot, picking out a small spot just in front of his ball, perhaps a single blade of grass that is in line with the faraway target, and aiming at that small spot. That is part of Jack's procedure in getting ready. Louise Suggs was like a machine, using the same alignment procedure with every club—just bing, bing, bing.

I developed my own procedure. I always approach the ball from behind to see where my target is. I then set the clubface behind the ball and step into my stance. It was explained to me that I needed to try to do the same thing every time, because feel changes from day to day.

It is also important to check your grip every now and then, because your grip can sometimes work into a bad position. You're not aware of it because your feel changes. For example, sometimes my hands get swollen and the grip just doesn't feel right, so I constantly check my grip.

Any number of things can throw your timing off, but your swing remains basically the same, as evidenced in photographs. Although your swing may feel awful that day, that's only because your tempo and timing are off. Hence everyone needs to develop a certain pattern.

That's also, I might add, why it's difficult for me to play slowly. I'm not geared for that. I'm already setting myself up for the shot, thinking about what I'm doing and getting into a rhythm of walking and playing, walking and playing. When I have to sit and wait between shots, I don't get into a real rhythm of the game, and it becomes more difficult to make a good swing.

It's very difficult when riding in electric or gasoline carts to get any rhythm. When I ride, which is seldom, I feel as if I'm always hurried because I'm so accustomed to using the time when I'm walking to a shot to think about what I'm doing and, if I miss the shot, why I missed it. I need enough time to discard that poor shot and think of what I'm going to do next.

You don't have that time in a golf cart, but you can still develop your own routine. Most golf courses today are quite crowded and you have a lot of time to wait between shots. Use that time constructively to think about your next shot, or why you missed the last one, and your game will improve.

TEMPO CHECKLIST

- Take the club back very smoothly, even slowly, the first 12 inches away from the ball.
- Develop a standard routine of lining up and addressing the ball —and stick to it!
- Use time between shots to plan your next shot or to contemplate why you missed the last one.

The Driver

The driver is the most important club in your bag. That old line, "Drive for show and putt for dough," really isn't relevant because you can't putt unless you get there and the driver is going to play the biggest role in getting you there.

The driver is the club that is going to put you in a good or bad position for your shot to the green. If you hit your tee shot well, you are setting yourself up mentally to play the hole well. If you hit the tee shot badly, you're setting yourself up to abandon ship.

A good drive can remove a ton of pressure from a golfer, make it easier to hit a second shot, and therefore take pressure off your putting. If you eliminate a good drive, you've wiped out the whole sequence.

Before you can become proficient off the tee, you have a difficult task: Remove any thought of distance. I am firmly convinced that your main objective off the tee is control, even if it means giving up some yardage. Once you think of control, you automatically put yourself in the frame of mind to hit a better tee shot. Lower-handicap golfers, by thinking of control, can put themselves in the frame of mind to *allow* a fade, which is a shot moving slightly left-to-right, or a draw, which moves slightly right-to-left.

Now you are aiming at a specific spot, rather than just banging away at any old place in the fairway. This is a big advantage. If you're able to place your drive in Position A on most fairways, your chances for a better score are much improved.

FOR MORE DISTANCE, EASY DOES IT

It can be really gratifying to hit a big tee shot, but you must understand that rather than sheer strength, long tee shots are the result

44

of good timing and balance resulting in solid contact with the ball. When I am getting maximum distance off the tee, I know that I'm not swinging hard at the ball but rather that my swing is under control and I am hitting the ball in the middle of the clubface. By raring back to get distance, we almost always throw our timing off. In fact, this affects the rest of your game in a subtle way. If you jump on a driver, you'll be inclined to jump on a 5-iron.

"Easy does it" spells control, but you also tend to hit the ball farther when you swing easy. The muscles are more lively and you'll notice more crispness in your shots.

I'm not suggesting that you don't hit the ball *hard* off the tee. You must hit it hard, but you must learn to hit it hard with control. The expression "Swing within yourself" can be valuable if you understand it.

A really full swing, one that is as hard as you can make it, would be a 100 percent swing. To swing "within yourself," then, would be about an 80 percent swing. That's taking a fairly hard cut at the ball, but it is controlled from within. Take a club and try it. You'll instantly feel as if you have better control over the club.

There's another reason for swinging within yourself. Players who always hit the ball hard, even on short iron shots, are players with virtually no feel for finesse shots, which I think of as real scoring shots. Swinging hard destroys feel. It's as simple as that.

The classic example of the player who swings within herself is the one who is never long with her shots, but always down the middle. She will wear you out over eighteen holes because she never puts herself into a position where she has an impossible shot.

THE SLICE

The slice is a national problem for golfers! I'm not talking about a fade, which is a highly controlled ball and one used by a number of the best professionals. I'm talking about the banana ball, that thing that takes up most of the fairway as it curves from left to right and seems to stand still in the air as it does so. A slice is an awful handicap, and an unnecessary one.

One of the causes of a slice is swinging too hard. Technically, it's caused by body movement—the body has moved through the hitting area too fast in its struggle to get clubhead speed. That automatically means that the clubface is open at impact. The club is simply swung so fast that the clubface doesn't have a chance to square up at impact. That's a matter of timing, too.

The opposite of the slice is the duck hook and it's caused by exactly the opposite action through the hitting area. The clubface comes through the impact area closed, and the ball spins to the left drastically.

SWINGING TOO HARD

What happens to the golf swing when you swing too hard? Generally, you pick your hands up too quickly as you take the club back, and your backswing has a tendency to be jerky. You've now eliminated any chance for getting all the way to the top of your backswing. Of course, that accounts for the fact that the body is moved too quickly. You subconsciously realize that you haven't reached the top of your backswing, and you compensate. You compensate by asking your body to do what the hands were supposed to do. This is a new adjustment for your swing, so it throws off your timing.

Your subconscious knows what your special timing is and what makes it happen. When you are off, your subconscious recognizes instantly that you are off that track and your body makes instantaneous adjustments. But they're not sufficient to restore your lost timing when you decided to hit the ball hard.

We see this happen in "hitting too fast." That's the very quick backswing and downswing that none of us like. I've had that problem myself and one consequence was that I hit a lot of shots fat, which is hitting behind the ball and catching too much grass. It all comes from being too fast at the top of your backswing.

ANALYZING YOUR OWN SWING

There are many clues given by your shots; I'd like everyone who reads this book to develop a talent for analyzing your own shots. It's amazing what a missed shot can tell you about your golf swing.

For example, a big slice is probably the result of coming over the top. If you are simply pushing the ball to the right of your target, without really hitting a slice, then usually the clubface is open when it comes into the ball. These clues suggest solutions. The slice would require a different swing plane, and the pushed ball would require only a change in tempo, one that allows the clubface to square up at impact.

As a general rule, men have a much bigger problem with the slice than women have. The reason is obvious. Men are much stronger from the waist up. They tend to use their arms a lot more than women do. Granted, they still can hit the ball a long way but it's usually true that they don't use their bodies nearly as much as women to generate power.

A little practice session will help you get rid of the slice. I suggest slowing your tempo somewhat. Although clubhead speed is important, you can change your tempo so that the clubface is more square at impact. Use your natural swing, but think in terms of making the angle of the clubface more square to the ball at impact. I think you'll notice that you have to slow your tempo somewhat to do this, and the squaring up probably will occur.

When I say "natural swing," I'm referring to everyone's natural rhythm. Use the tempo or rhythm that is your own.

DEVELOPING YOUR GAME FROM THE TEE

If you have trouble with your driver, I suggest a trick I've sometimes used on the tour. Switch to a 3-wood or 4-wood for a couple of rounds for your tee shots. You'll often find that you'll hit farther with those woods than you did with your driver.

The instant you pull out one of those clubs, the idea of distance is gone and control dominates. Usually, you're paired with another player, and when you use a fairway wood off the tee, you are simply striving for accuracy and no longer in a competition to see who will hit the longest drive.

Without question, I would recommend a practice tee regime in which you teach yourself what your proper tempo really is when the ball goes relatively straight. Out of that will come the vital control.

The number one requirement for becoming a good driver is to get the idea of power out of your head. By controlling that impulse, you'll give yourself a new degree of control. A badly controlled drive automatically puts on the player a kind of pressure that is almost impossible to handle. You are suddenly confronted with unanticipated trouble shots. You are no longer able to play in a relaxed way. Controlled shots are the key.

DRIVER CHECKLIST

- Forget power, think of control.
- Aim at a specific spot.
- Swing smoothly and concentrate on solid contact.
- To correct a slice, slow your swing tempo and concentrate on hitting the ball with a square clubface.
- To correct troubled tee shots, occasionally switch to a fairway wood off the tee.

The Mystery of Long-Iron Play

The long irons are considered to be the most difficult clubs to play of all the clubs in the bag. Personally, I enjoy playing long-iron shots and would like you to enjoy them too. The long irons—the 2-iron, 3-iron, and 4-iron—are not as difficult to swing as you might think, but they do have specific requirements.

Although shorter irons can be more forgiving, I like the long irons because they're excellent clubs to use for hitting special shots, such as low shots from under trees and shots in the wind. Because there's less loft on these clubs, you can hit the ball lower, which is their utility aspect. For example, if the wind is high you can really have much more control over the ball with these clubs by simply hitting low, running shots that will be relatively unaffected by a stiff breeze.

Most amateurs have a problem with their long irons. I believe it's because they don't play enough. They seem to feel they have to force these clubs, using sheer muscle to lift the ball up into the air instead of allowing the loft of the club to get the ball up.

The simplest tip I can give a woman amateur for long-iron play is to just move the ball a bit more forward in the stance, put a good swing on it, and let the club do the job.

While this may seem overly simplified, it's the one key to long-iron play that is often ignored. Because amateurs seldom think of long-iron play in this manner, they lose confidence in these clubs. Every time they drag them out of their bags, they feel as if they won't hit the shot. Consequently, they don't. For that reason, most amateurs turn to higher lofted fairway woods, like the 5-wood, 6-wood, and 7-wood. Still, it would be nice to have a choice. So here are a few tips for hitting long irons.

48

Ball position is one of the most important keys to good long-iron play. Play the ball to the left of the center of your stance.

If you learn to play long irons, you can add extra finesse to your game. For myself, it would just break my heart if I had to give up my 2-iron. I feel that I can maneuver the ball better with that club than almost any other. Additionally, I often use a 2-iron off the tee for better control.

THE PSYCHOLOGY OF LONG-IRON PLAY

There's a great deal of psychology in long-iron play. The way that the club appears as it sits behind the ball makes most players want to overpower this shot. You look down and you don't see very much clubhead. The blade is less lofted and smaller than the clubheads of other irons, so you can see only the top of the blade behind the ball. The result is the feeling that something needs to be added. Unfortunately, that addition is usually an attempt to muscle the ball.

Long irons are seldom used and golfers generally tend to be a bit leery of them. Golfers hear a lot of negative things about long irons, which produces an even more negative attitude. However, *the swing is basically the same with long irons and fairway woods*.

If a golfer swung as smoothly and easily with a 2-iron as with a 5-wood, she would hit it just as well. So the basic problem with these clubs is a psychological one. It's important to repeat this fact to yourself because it's one of the true secrets of good long-iron play. The more you can absorb this thought, the better player you will become.

It's also important to remember that these clubs have been carefully and expertly engineered. They will do their job, if you just *allow* them to. If you try to add something, you will cancel all the engineering built into this club. Thinking about this seriously is critical in playing long irons successfully.

POINTERS FOR LONG-IRON PLAY

There are two major tips for good long-iron play. First, it is not necessary to change your swing for the long irons. Second, the position of the ball at address must be correct. Not changing your swing speaks for itself. Ball position, however, needs a more thorough explanation.

For the short irons, the pitching wedge, 9-iron, and somewhat for the 8-iron, the ball should be positioned in the center of your stance. From that position, there is a progression of the ball position toward the left foot as the clubs get longer. The reason is that the longer the club, the later in the swing the bottom of its arc occurs.

The ball should be played where that arc touches the ground. With long irons, because the bottom of the arc occurs later, it occurs more to the left in the stance. That's why the ball position should be moved more toward the left foot as the clubs get longer. The long irons should be played closer to the left heel than to the center of the stance.

THERE ARE NO EASY ANSWERS

As I write this, I'm reminded how often I am asked about long-iron play by my amateur partners in Pro-Ams. Although they often have difficulty with long irons, they're stubborn about them and want me to tell them what they should do to force themselves to learn to play these clubs.

Of course, I have no pat answer. I have no pat answer for any club, for that matter. Such an answer would go against everything I believe about good golf, which is that there are no absolutes!

However, you must set the stage correctly for good long-iron play. I'm talking about fundamentals. You will not be a good long-iron player if your grip, swing, and alignment are incorrect. *The way to master these fundamentals is with your own teaching professional.*

Here's a routine that will help you hit better long irons: On the practice tee, hit a lot of long-iron shots and, *on every shot*, hit the ball as if you had a 6-iron in your hand with the expectation that the shot will go only as far as your 6-iron would go.

It sounds simple, doesn't it? It isn't. For some reason, probably impatience, it's quite hard to continue to hit long irons on the practice tee as if they were middle irons. It's only natural to feel, as you watch these shots go out in such a surprisingly good way, that if you're getting good results with such an easy swing, then why not just add something and get more spectacular results. It doesn't work that way. I know you won't believe me. Still, in all humility, that is the way to learn how to play long irons.

There are no miracles. Try to swing smoothly and hit the ball solidly, but not far. This will give you the feel of the club. From there, you have an opportunity to build your confidence in these clubs. This is the swing you are going to use for the 6-iron and it is also the swing you are going to use for the 2-iron.

Ultimately, of course, you must take this practice to the golf course. I recommend that you try not only to master this feeling on the practice tee, but that you persist with rather lengthy practice in order to make it so automatic that, when you have a real shot on the golf course, you don't revert to your old ways. One of the major points about any kind of practice is how you take it into combat!

Although there are no easy answers, these basic thoughts should help you be a better long-iron player.

LONG-IRON CHECKLIST

- Remember, it's the *fear* of long irons that makes them difficult to hit.
- Check your fundamentals: grip, stance, alignment.
- Ball position is crucial: Play long irons closer to your left heel than to the center of your stance.
- Practice hitting a long iron as if it were a 6-iron.
- Don't try to muscle the ball. Concentrate on a smooth swing and let the engineering of the club do the work.

Chipping

Although women do not have as much strength as men in their upper
bodies, arms, or hands, they can still play with a lot of feel around
the green. Women who are good at chip shots and pitch shots can
play and score well. I'm a firm believer that if the average player
uses the right technique and the right fundamentals, she can learn
these shots.

The technique I advocate will work with any club. In fact, it
works with the whole swing! If you absorb this technique in chipping, it will work with the big swing since, in chipping, you use
the same positions as in the full swing. Your club is in the same
position, it's just a smaller swing.

Throughout my career, I have always favored the use of a pitch-
and-run shot—letting the ball hit on the green and run to the hole
—rather than a lofted shot, unless there's no other choice. If you
must hit over a bunker, then use a softer, more lofted shot. The
pitch-and-run is a great scoring tool. One of the most important
factors in this shot is club selection, which involves knowing what
each club will do.

Chipping is definitely a feel shot, but you have to know the
characteristics of the clubs. With a lofted club, the ball goes higher.
With a less-lofted club, the ball has a lower trajectory and will run
more.

If you are just a couple of feet from the edge of the green, it's
not going to take a lot of effort to carry a 7-iron to the putting
surface and let it run to the hole. You're not going to have to hit
it that hard because the shot will have enough force to carry to the
hole.

If you're farther back, say 10 yards from the green, and you use a 5-, 6-, or 7-iron, you're going to have to hit the ball so hard to carry such a distance that the lower trajectory club will cause the ball to run over the green. It will have too much force on it. So, maybe you should use an 8- or 9-iron, which would give you enough loft to get to the edge of the green and roll to the hole.

There are two rules of thumb for pitching. One is to use the club with which you can carry the ball to the green and let it roll to the hole. The other technique, and this is what I generally use, is to choose the club that will carry the ball *halfway* to the hole, then let it roll the rest of the way.

This technique works best if the green's surface is fairly consistent and level. I use this a lot because I know that I'll get the ball at least halfway to the hole.

For example, if I have a 30-foot chip from the fringe, rather than take a 7- or 8-iron and carry to the edge of the green, I'll probably take a 9-iron and carry the shot halfway to the hole, letting it run the rest of the way. That's a shot I've worked on. Pitching and chipping are feel shots, and that's why you must work on these shots more than you work on full shots.

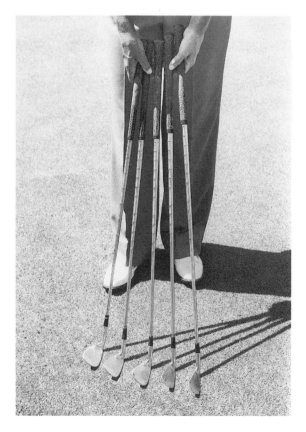

By comparing various irons, you can see how their lofts differ. The short irons have the most loft; the long irons have the least.

I learned these shots when I was sixteen or seventeen years old. The little putting green at Jal Country Club had a cement block wall around it, about a foot high, with an iron railing above the concrete. I could either pitch over the railing or under it, so I'd practice different shots, going over, then going through the opening. I got a good feel for which club to hit and how hard to hit it.

Growing up in west Texas, I learned to use the pitch-and-run. We hardly ever used the pitching wedge or sand wedge because our greens were so firm and so small that we usually ran the ball in. I became very proficient with my 9-iron. I very rarely hit a soft shot. I would use my 9-iron and close the face slightly to hit a little firmer shot that would run. Or, I would open the blade slightly and get a little softer shot. I might play a lot of different shots with just one club. As it turned out, the 9-iron became my favorite club for chipping.

Again, by knowing what I was trying to accomplish, and knowing what each club would do, I learned to play the shot well.

FUNDAMENTALS OF CHIPPING

The same basic grip is used for chipping as for any other club. The stance, however, is different. One thing that hurts the average woman player is that she puts her feet too far apart, taking a stance that is too wide for this shot. This creates a bigger than necessary weight shift and turn for the short distance.

Make sure your stance is a narrow one, with your feet no more than five or six inches apart. This can vary slightly, but the stance should be narrow enough to take the weight shift out of the shot. A good practice technique is to keep all of your weight on the left side at address. Don't shift your weight. You want the left side to dominate the swing. The left side is going to be your guide throughout the shot.

You also need to make sure you hit down on the ball. In order to do this, the ball is usually played in the center of the stance or slightly right of center. Many times people try to hit *up* on the ball when they chip and they get very wristy and top it, blade it, or chunk it. There's no force behind the shot.

To put a little backspin on the ball and have control over the shot, hit down on it. You must drive down into the shot, rather than try to pick it up. That's why the loft of the club helps. If you're using a 9-iron, the ball will get up. You don't have to help it up. Let the club do that. Many times, women will try to pick the ball out of the grass. Instead, stay on your left side, play the ball down, and drive the club down into the shot.

Address a pitch shot with a narrow stance. Play the ball in the center, or right of center, in your stance. Your hands should be even with, or slightly ahead of, the ball.

The shoulders, hips, and feet are slightly open to the target.

Because this shot is mainly arms, shoulders, and hands, hand position at address is one of the important fundamentals. By playing the ball in the center of the stance, or slightly back of center, and by keeping the weight on the left side, the hands will be at least even with or slightly ahead of the ball. However, the hands should be no farther ahead than the center of the left thigh. This hand position will enable you to come into the ball with a more sharply descending blow, which will give you a crisp and controlled shot.

TECHNIQUE

A lot of people ask me how to put backspin on the ball. That's not difficult if your ball is in a good lie, that is, if it's not buried in deep grass or lodged in a divot. Most people are unable to put spin on the ball because they try to hit the shot with their hands alone; they get handsy and loose wristed. They collapse their wrists instead of hitting through the shot with firm action.

You must be very firm through the hitting area—but with a small swing. Anytime you're using less than a full swing, which you're certainly doing on a pitch shot, you're dealing with feel. In order to get a good feel for the shot, the length of your backswing and follow-through *must* be equal.

56

You must be firm through the shot—firm hands and firm wrists.

The average player will often take a huge backswing when hitting a shot of only 20 yards. Then, natural feel takes over. Subconsciously they recognize that they will hit this ball over the green with this big swing, so they slow down the clubhead speed. When they get to the ball, there's no clubhead speed at all! The average player then whips the club with the hands and meets disaster, either hitting the shot fat, or blading it.

On a small swing, stay firm through the hitting area. Be consistent. The follow-through should be no longer and no shorter than the backswing. Also, if you keep the left side strong and moving through the shot, you'll have a better chance of making a good shot.

AIM

In playing a pitch shot, you should concentrate on a small area of the green. This is the spot you've selected to which you want to carry the ball. You should concentrate on this spot, or area, but you should also be thinking *toward* the hole. This will help give you a good feel for the amount of force needed to make the ball roll to the hole.

Many times, players who are trying to pitch over a bunker will think only of the carry. Since they are basically thinking of the bunker, their natural feel takes over and, plunk, they're in the bunker. Instead, think *past* the bunker and to the green.

The backswing and the follow-through should be symmetrical—of equal length.

PITCHING WITH THE WEDGE AND SAND WEDGE

The same fundamentals apply to using a wedge or sand wedge for pitching. You must still use a narrow stance but, the longer the shot, the wider the stance, because you are trying to hit the shot with a little more force.

I also use a slightly open stance with the wedge. This helps me keep the bottom of the blade, or clubface, going right toward the target, rather than allowing the wrists to roll over, as on the follow-through in a full swing. This keeps the ball going straight, just like a putt.

Your wrists should be firm. Don't try to create a releasing of the hands because that can cause you to collapse and chunk, blade, or shank it. Your wrists should not be stiff, just firm. You've got to have some clubhead feel. As in other shots, the left side must be firm and in the lead throughout the shot.

CHIPPING AND PITCHING CHECKLIST

- Practice the pitch-and-run using various clubs.
- Use a narrow stance.
- Address the shot with your weight on the left side and keep it there.
- Play the ball in the center of your stance, or slightly right of center.
- At address, your hands should be even with the ball or slightly ahead.
- Hit down on the shot, keeping your wrists firm.
- Use a small swing with a backswing and follow-through of equal length.
- With a wedge or sand wedge, use a slightly open stance and don't let the wrists roll over through the shot.

Taking the Fear out of Bunker Shots

When you're in a bunker, what you're basically trying to do is just get out. The more you practice, the more adept you can become at how hard to hit the ball. Then the bunker shot becomes a fun shot to play.

One of the keys to good bunker play is having a sand wedge. It's not imperative but it certainly helps.

Sand wedges have been specifically designed for hitting out of the sand. One of the most difficult things about hitting out of bunkers is going too deeply into the sand with the club. It's not so much that the golfer hits too far behind the ball, she usually just digs too deeply. Even if the golfer hits only an inch behind the ball, she will dig too far into the sand if she is using a pitching wedge or 9-iron. Then, she cannot get the ball up and cannot really follow through.

A true sand wedge has a wide flange on the bottom of the club. The flange, or sole, of the club is wider and flatter than in other irons and prevents digging too deeply. Instead, the sand wedge helps you to sort of flatten out your swing when you hit down into the shot. You just scoop underneath the ball; consequently the club is able to come through the shot and you can better follow through. That's why I advocate a sand wedge.

There are many, many kinds of sand wedges. You just have to find one that you like. They're all designed to keep you from digging too much into the sand with the club.

The sand wedge will also be your most lofted club, so it will not carry very far, even if you hit a full shot. At the most, I will hit a full sand wedge only about 50 or 60 yards on a shot from the fairway.

60

For bunker shots, use a sand wedge (at left). It has a much wider flange than the pitching wedge (center), or a 9-iron (at right).

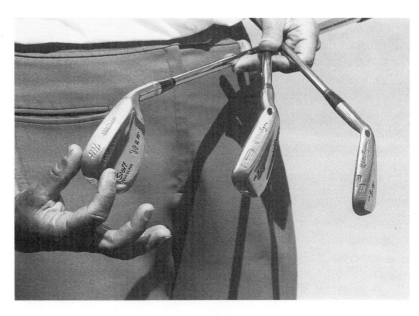

Women have a difficult time getting out of the sand because they must make a bigger swing. Men have a better chance at this shot because they're stronger and can use less swing. Any time less effort is used, a golfer is going to be better at a particular shot. However, bunker play is difficult for most golfers, although it does not have to be.

The design of modern golf courses makes bunker play more difficult than in the past. In earlier days, and on many of our finest old courses, the bunkers were right next to the green. Today, bunkers are constructed quite a distance from the green to allow room for mowing the fringe. So now we have longer bunker shots on these newer courses. To me, those are the most difficult shots to play because you must carry the ball a long way and make a much bigger swing. You cannot really finesse the ball.

THE FUNDAMENTALS

A routine bunker shot demands a blast shot or cut shot. For this shot, open the blade of the club a little and then take your grip. DO NOT take your grip and then open the blade. That will not work because your hands will revert back to a square position and will square up the blade. For this shot, you want a slightly open blade for a softer shot.

Play the ball just a little left of center in your stance. You want to cut underneath the ball, and this ball position will give you a better chance.

In a bunker, open the blade a bit, then take your grip. Here's what an open blade looks like.

You don't want to contact the ball first in a blast shot because it is the sand that will take the ball out of the bunker on the follow-through.

The ball needs to come out high, because you usually need to clear the lip of the bunker, but you want to get the ball up without *trying* to make it go up. Do not try to lift the ball; it will get up by itself if you play the shot correctly.

After opening the blade of the club, aim your body and shoulders to the left of the target before taking your stance. You also need to aim to the left of the target because you are hitting a cut shot and the ball will normally kick to the right when it lands, since it has a left-to-right spin on it.

THE SWING FROM THE BUNKER

Swing the club on the line of your shoulders and feet. Do not take the club away on the outside. Take it straight away. It will feel as if you're taking it outside because, with your body open, you will be taking it on a straight line *in relation to your body.*

However, if you want to put a lot of cut on the ball or if you want it to stop very quickly, you can take the club away slightly on the outside.

There is one terrific tip for the average player on bunker shots. When you hit from a bunker and come through the shot, do not roll your wrists over as you would on a normal shot from the fairway. Your hands should not pronate—it's almost like a block shot. Most

For a standard bunker shot, the ball position should be left of center. Hips, shoulders, and feet are aligned to the left of the target. The stance is wider than usual, and your feet should be slightly dug in for better footing. Hands are even with the ball.

assuredly the left side, once again, must follow through first, and the back of the left hand should face the sky on the follow-through. This keeps the blade open all the way through the shot, so that the ball will land very softly. When you follow through there should not be a lot of force behind it.

In a bunker, align your feet, hips, and shoulders to the left of the target, as you would in an open stance.

This alignment allows you to swing the club back on a line with your body.

On a standard bunker shot, when you come through the ball, don't roll your wrists over. Keep the back of the left hand facing the sky.

ANOTHER WAY TO PLAY BUNKER SHOTS

There's another relatively easy way to play sand shots. I'm not as adept at this, but it's a simple way to get out of bunkers.

Most people have a terrific fear of bunkers because they think they must hit behind the ball and do a number of things they don't usually do when striking a golf ball. However, if you let the club do the work for you, take just a little bit of sand, and follow through, once you learn the basic method it's an easy shot.

Many people believe they must take sand first and they just dig right down into the ground. They hit behind the ball and they hit a lot of sand, but they've dug so deeply that they can never get out. With a sand wedge, if you take just enough sand between the clubhead and the ball, then follow through, the ball will come right out. You will never fear this shot again if you do that one simple thing.

Take enough sand between the ball and the club so that the club does not touch the ball. This is what some people refer to as a shovel shot.

Take a fairly long swing. Most golfers believe that if they take a big swing they will hit the ball over the green. That's not true because the sand wedge has a lot of loft on it. The sand will also slow down the clubhead speed, so you will not hit the ball too far.

If you face a really long bunker shot, you must take a big swing and very little sand and really try to put some force behind it.

However, most of the time you'll have a 20-yard or 25-yard shot. This doesn't take a really big swing but it *does* take more swing than you would use on a chip shot of the same distance.

Many people take a tiny little backswing, then they don't get out of the bunker. You don't get out of a bunker because you aren't using enough force. This occurs because the sand slows the clubhead. Some types of sand are heavier than other types, so in heavy sand you must use even more force.

You can learn how heavy the sand is when you step into the bunker. Although you cannot ground your club—rest it in the sand before you start your backswing, which is against the Rules of Golf—you can feel the sand with your feet when you take your stance and get set.

Usually, when chipping, we use a narrow little stance. In the bunker, you might widen your stance so that you have firmer footing.

You don't want to use a lot of body action. This is mainly a hands and arms shot. It does not require a big shoulder turn, just a slight shoulder turn, and you stand almost flat-footed. If you try to use your feet and legs too much, you're liable to lose your footing and blade the ball, which means you hit too much of the ball and not enough sand.

I've included this photo to give you a better mental picture of the clubhead at impact. The blade comes into the ball and, like a shovel, takes a very shallow scoop of sand.

THE SOFT SHOT

The soft sand shot is used when you don't have to hit a bunker shot a great distance and when you want the ball to land softly and not run very far. On this shot, the ball will normally take one bounce and have some backspin.

Open the blade slightly, then take your grip.

To hit the soft sand shot, take a big backswing in slow motion and maintain a good follow-through. The momentum of the swing will carry the ball out of the bunker.

Because you are hitting a soft shot, take a bit more sand than usual as you hit the ball, but you still must maintain some clubhead speed through the shot. I prefer to take a fairly large swing, more of an easy arm swing, and maintain the follow-through to get the ball out.

Swing the club back along the line of your feet, shoulders, and hips.

Take a fairly long backswing. Don't use a lot of body action; this is mainly an arms-and-hands shot.

The blade is still open as you come into the ball.

The blade does not turn over through the shot.

Be sure to follow through.

THE RUNNING BUNKER SHOT

The principles of the standard bunker shot apply to the running bunker shot, with a few exceptions. Use a more square clubface, rather than an open blade. Play the ball more in the center of the stance, rather than left of center. You're still going to contact the sand first, but you want the ball to come out of the bunker at a lower trajectory without much spin on it, so that it will run part of the distance to the hole.

PLAYING FROM A BURIED OR FRIED-EGG LIE

The buried lie is, obviously, when the ball is somewhat buried in the sand. A so-called fried-egg lie is when the ball sits in the middle of the large imprint that was made when the ball struck the sand. The lie looks like a fried egg, with the ball acting as the egg's yolk.

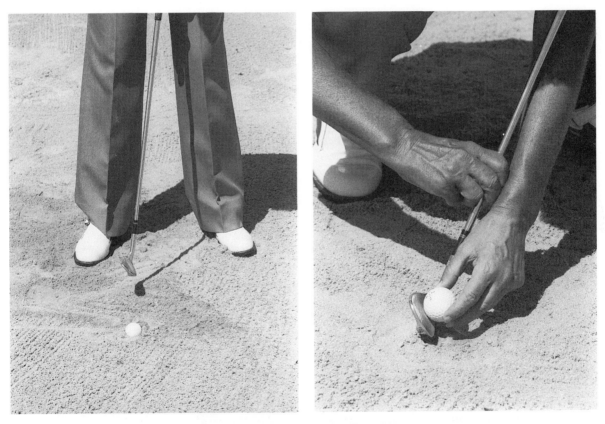

When facing a buried lie, play the ball more toward the back of your stance. Close the clubface slightly, then take your grip.

This picture shows how the ball reacts when you use a closed clubface in a buried or fried-egg lie in a bunker. The ball will climb up the face at impact, and pop out of the bunker.

But there's nothing tasty about this shot—it's very, very difficult. All you're trying to do with this shot is get the ball out of the bunker and somewhere on the green.

I play buried and fried-egg shots in the same way. The safest method is to close the blade of the sand wedge slightly, then take your grip. Play the ball in the center of the stance.

I concentrate a great deal on contacting the sand behind the ball. It's so important not to strike the ball first in order to avoid driving the ball into the bunker more deeply.

Use a more descending blow than you usually would, and the ball will just climb out of the bunker. The follow-through is not as important as usual, although you should try to follow through. This shot will run because it will have a much lower trajectory when it comes out of the bunker.

As you become a proficient player, you'll have a better chance to play this shot accurately, but what you will always be trying to do is get the ball out of the sand so that you will not have to play another bunker shot.

WHEN YOUR BALL IS UNDER THE LIP

Occasionally, your ball will become embedded under the lip of a bunker. Again, your objective in playing this shot is just to get out. If the ball is buried to the point where you can't even see it, the best thing to do is to declare the ball unplayable. The Rules of Golf allow you to drop it at the nearest point of relief, within the bunker, with a one-stroke penalty.

If the ball is only half-buried under the lip of the bunker, the best way to play it is similar to the way you would play a buried lie in the sand. Close the clubface, then take your grip. Take a solid stance in the sand by wiggling your feet a bit as you dig in.

You will usually have an uphill lie when the ball is embedded under the lip, so try to keep your body as level as possible. Hit the sand slightly behind the ball. The club will act almost like a shovel, and the ball usually goes straight up because you are driving the ball into the bank; the bank acts almost as a wall, and forces the ball back into the clubface. The ball then climbs up the clubface and, hopefully, out of the bunker. The ball will pop straight up. It will not go very far, but at least you are out. Do not try to follow through, because you will not be able to from this position.

You are unlucky to face this shot. In my clinics I tell golfers that if they continually get lies like this, maybe they should just quit!

THE DOWNHILL LIE IN A BUNKER

The bunker shot from a downhill lie is one of the worst shots in golf, along with the long bunker shot. Usually it means your ball is in the back of the bunker and you are faced with a long carry. Because of the downhill lie, it is difficult to get the ball up in the air to make this long carry. Additionally, if you have a downhill lie it usually means that your ball is against the bunker's back lip, forcing you to pick the club straight up so that your club won't hit the sand or the lip on your backswing, costing a penalty stroke.

To play this type of shot, play the ball in the center, or right of center, in your stance. Use a square blade, rather than an open

When the ball is under the lip of the bunker, close the clubface, then take your grip. Play the ball right of center in your stance.

To play a ball under the lip of the bunker, take a fairly long backswing.

Hit into the bank. Don't try to hit the ball on the upswing; hit it on the downswing, contacting the sand slightly behind the ball. You won't hurt your hands with this method. You won't be able to follow through on this shot.

blade, so that you won't hit the ball straight right. Address the shot with your hands farther ahead of the ball than usual, because you must break your wrists abruptly, especially if you're against the bunker's back lip.

The force for this shot comes mainly from your hands. On the backswing, cock your wrists almost immediately. On the downswing, take a little bit of sand and follow through as much as you can. This means you are taking a fairly big swing and a big follow-through in order to give the shot height and length. The ball will run, so you're just trying to get the ball out, rather than waste another shot in the bunker.

This shot is so difficult that it may be more prudent sometimes to turn around and hit the ball to the side, rather than trying to hit to the green. If you feel that you cannot hit this shot, then your best choice is to just pitch out to the side or even to the back.

When facing a downhill lie in a bunker, use a square blade, play the ball to the right of the center of your stance. Address the ball with your hands slightly ahead of the ball.

Pick up the club abruptly on the backswing.

On the downswing, contact the sand first.

You'll need a long follow-through on this shot.

Don't forget to rake the bunker. It's important to be courteous to other golfers. That's part of the game.

STANDARD BUNKER-SHOT CHECKLIST

- Use a sand wedge.
- Open the blade slightly, then take your grip.
- Use a wider stance than normal.
- Play ball left of center in stance.
- Aim body slightly to the left of the target.
- Use an arm and hands swing with no weight shift.
- Take just a small amount of sand as you hit the ball.
- Don't roll your wrists over as you hit through the ball.
- Be sure to follow through, unless your ball is under the lip of the bunker.

The Fundamentals of Putting

By some standards, I've been a pretty good putter throughout my career. My own theory about good putting, however, may be a little different than that of other players. A lot of very fine putters have always felt that putting is one game and the striking of the ball on long shots is another game, but I've always related putting to the big swing. If my swing is under control and I'm hitting the ball well, I'm going to putt well.

Putting is just a smaller version of the big swing. If you have a bad grip, you'll probably have a bad grip when putting, too. You will do the same maneuvers putting, and make the same technical mistakes, that you do on long shots. Very few players look at putting in this way, but this view has worked for me.

I can analyze my golf swing and figure out why I'm not hitting the ball crisply, and almost always that solution works right down to my putting. That's one reason I've never practiced putting as much as do many tournament players. Also, I seldom practice on the putting green. Putting is all feel. No two greens are exactly alike and no lie on the green is exactly like any other, so you don't get the same feel on a practice putting green as you do while playing. My technique has been to practice my putting during my regular practice rounds. During the practice round I'll chip and putt a bit from different angles and that's about it.

This is difficult for the average player because the pace of play on your home course usually means that you'd better just play a hole and get out of the way! But the techniques I'm going to give you in this chapter can be applied to your own stroke on a practice putting green or on your living room carpet.

Putting is probably the most individual part of the game. Everyone has their own style. However, just as in the big swing, there are certain fundamentals that all good putters share.

THE GRIP AND STANCE

In putting, the palms face one another and are square to the target. The hands must stay close together so that they can work together.

You should also try to have your two hands as close together as possible. They should fit together even more snugly than they do when gripping longer clubs.

When you take your stance, if you feel more comfortable with your weight mostly on your left foot, you should play the ball more off the left foot. However, if your weight is equally distributed between your right and left sides, play the ball in the center of your

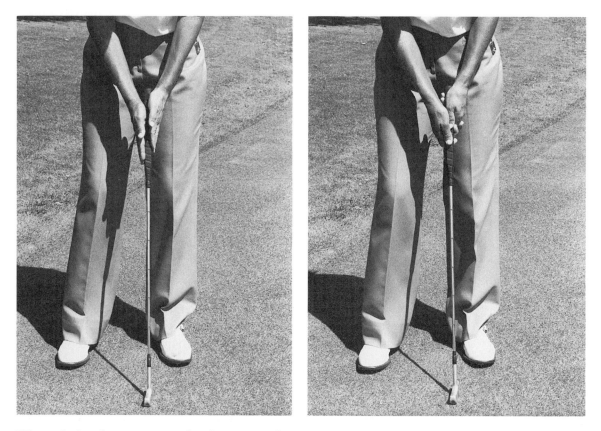

When gripping the putter, my palms face one another and are square to the target.

This is my putting grip. My hands fit snugly together. I use a regular overlapping grip, just as I do in the full swing.

stance. If your weight is mostly on your right foot, then play the ball off of your right foot. This will put your head over the ball.

Your eyes must be directly over the ball. If you bend too far over the ball, you will have a tendency to pull your putts to the left. If you're standing too far from the ball, your eyes will fall to the inside, rather than right over the ball, and you'll probably push most of your putts to the right.

A good way to visualize this is to think of a ball at the end of a string. If you're in a good position, you could hold the end of the string under your eyes and the ball would swing back and forth on a straight line over the line of the putt.

I sometimes check the position of my eyes by holding the end of my putter grip under my eyes and letting the putter hang straight down. If the end of the putter hangs directly over the ball, then my head is in the right position.

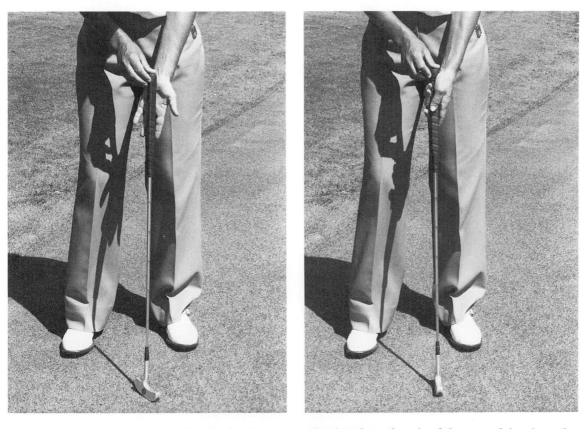

Another key to good putting is to keep the grip of the putter lying down the center of the palm of the left hand.

Golfers have different putting styles. If you play the ball toward the left side of your stance, keep most of your weight on your left side so that your eyes are over the ball. If you play the ball toward the right side, keep most of your weight there.

Your eyes should be directly over the ball. You can check this by hanging your putter straight down from your eyes.

THE STROKE

There are all types of putting strokes. Some good putters use their wrists and hands a lot, some use their hands and arms, and still others use only their arms or shoulders. Again, they all have one thing in common; they're trying to achieve a pendulum-style stroke so that the blade will move straight back and straight through on the imaginary line on which we want the ball to travel.

Good putters don't move over the ball. Sometimes, I can stand over a putt, see the line, and visualize the ball going into the hole. So, if I start to miss the putts, I know that I'm moving. If you have already checked your eye position, grip, and alignment, and you're still missing a lot of putts that you should be making, nine times out of ten you're moving at some point in your stroke. One way to stop movement in your putting stroke is to practice watching the putter blade hit the ball before you look up.

Any kind of movement can throw you off. If your eyes follow the putter blade back and forth during the stroke, or if you look up too quickly, you will not putt consistently well. You may make a few putts, but you'll miss more than you should. Make sure that you're very steady throughout your stroke.

Curtis Strange is a good example of a player who is very steady over his putts. You can see that his head does not come up until the ball is almost to the hole on short putts, or until the ball is about

When your eyes are directly over the ball, as in these three photographs, you have a better opportunity of making a perpendicular stroke, one that goes straight back and straight through.

halfway to the hole on long putts. That's probably how Curtis makes sure that he stays steady while putting.

LENGTH OF STROKE

Just as with the big swing, you want the speed of the clubhead to have its greatest momentum at impact.

If you took a long backswing for a short putt, your instincts would tell you that if you made a big follow-through you would hit the ball over the green. So, you will tend to slow the putter blade at impact. You may actually stop the blade at the ball for fear that you're going to hit the putt too far. You are slowing the momentum of the putter head just when it should be at its fullest.

It's important to have a symmetrical stroke—the length of the follow-through should be identical to the length of the backswing. If you go to extremes—for example, if you have a very long follow-through—you'll have a tendency to make a short backswing, and vice versa.

It's very difficult to develop good putting feel with that type of stroke. Of course, feel is what putting is all about. This principle applies throughout your game; full swing, half-swing, pitch, chip, or putt. If you take the club back shoulder high, then your follow-through should be shoulder high. If you take it back waist high, then your follow-through should be waist high. If your back swing is six inches long, your follow-through should be six inches long. That is the way a pendulum swings.

USEFUL PUTTING ADVICE

As with other parts of your game, when you practice putting, check your fundamentals. Throughout your game it's very difficult to create a good swing with a bad grip or with other poor fundamentals. If you have a weak grip in the big swing, for instance, it is difficult to take the club back to the inside, so it's pointless for a teacher to tell you to take the club back more inside. Your poor grip will not allow that. You must first develop your fundamentals and your putting stroke.

You need to be as comfortable as possible over a putt. Tension, I believe, is the worst enemy in putting. If you point your finger, for example, you don't think about it, you just do it. This is basically the same with putting. Sometimes when you're under pressure, you just have to trust what you have, and not think of mechanics. Just hit it! Say to yourself, "I'm going to hit this towards the hole . . ." Many times, you'll make it without even thinking about it.

If tension makes you miss a putt, you've probably become too mechanical or too stroke conscious while you're over the putt. When you try to *make* a stroke happen, it never does. You cannot think just of mechanics, or you'll forget something else. When you're on the green in a tournament situation, you've got to be thinking of the break or the speed of the green. The only mechanical thing you can really worry about is your alignment. After that, all you can do is decide where you want the ball to go.

In my years on the Tour, I never thought of making or missing a putt. I never stood over a putt and thought, ''I've *got* to make this putt.'' I wouldn't be over that putt if I didn't want to make it! Instead, just think, ''If I'm going to have any chance of making this putt, I've got to do certain things.''

Concentrate on those ''things'' rather than trying to coach yourself by thinking that you must make the putt. That's when you get a lot of tension and have a terrible time—you'll jerk the stroke or move or try what is called the wish stroke (you try to wish the ball into the hole instead of stroking it into the hole).

Try to develop a repetitive putting stroke—something you can depend on. Your feel changes all the time, so it may feel as if your stroke changes. Actually, it doesn't change at all. On a given day or situation, although your timing may be off and you may not stroke the ball quite solidly, you can still be in fairly good control of the ball if you have developed a consistent stroke. That's what makes all the great players as great as they are.

FORGET AGGRESSION ON THE GREEN

When I hear the phrase, ''Never up, never in,'' I just cringe! It's supposed to encourage you to putt firmly, but I think it may cause you to knock the ball way past the hole. Betsy Rawls was one of the best putters I ever saw—this woman never three-putted! She gave me a great tip that I have used throughout my career: ''Ball to the hole,'' which is what she thought while putting.

By putting the ball *to* the hole, rather than trying to ram it into the back of the cup, you can use the sides of the cup and the ''corners.'' If the ball is rolling with too much force, you can't do that; then you have to hit it dead straight in the center.

A straight putt is one of the most difficult to hit because you have no room for error. With a breaking putt, you can use the entire hole. If you stroke it at the top of the cup, you have the whole lower lip of the cup to work with. But, if you stroke a straight putt too hard, and it hits the lip of the hole, it won't go in. Likewise, if you stroke a breaking putt too firmly, the force of the stroke won't let the ball fall in the corners.

Remember, if the ball just rolls to the hole and no farther, and hits the lip, it could fall in.

PUTTING CHECKLIST

- Address the putt with your eyes directly over the ball.
- Don't move your eyes, head, or body during the stroke.
- Develop a pendulum-style stroke with a backswing and follow-through of equal length.
- When playing, don't *think* of the mechanics of the stroke; just putt the ball!
- Don't putt too aggressively—stroke the ball to die at the hole.

Beware of Golf's Cliches

Golf, more than most games, has a number of cliches, often successfully disguised as "tips." Watch out! Unless you understand these cliches, even a well-meaning partner can cause you to develop very bad swing habits with a generously offered tip.

Golfers tend to grasp at straws, often out of sheer desperation. These cliches are the straws and it has been my observation that golfers do themselves damage by believing these so-called truths or by not understanding what the phrases really mean. I'll review ten cliches and what they really mean.

1. STAY BEHIND THE BALL

I'll start with a common one: Stay behind the ball.

This is potentially confusing. The most common misinterpretation causes the golfer to stay completely on the right foot on the downswing, which brings disaster.

When you swing correctly, you actually feel as if you are staying behind the ball, but your body is actually moving toward the target. The weight shifts *toward* the target. "Staying behind the ball" refers to timing. The weight should shift forward *at impact*. If the weight is ahead of the ball at that moment, then it's too far toward the target at the wrong time. Yes, the weight should be behind the ball *but it should be shifting as impact occurs.*

Without that shifting action, your weight remains on the back foot, which leads to inconsistent play.

The weight shift actually comes from the lower part of the body, from the waist down. The weight shift starts with the hips and the feet, while the upper part of the body stays fairly still on the back-swing. The upper body stays on the same level. On the downswing, you swing the club down through the shot with your arms and upper body. You accomplish this by allowing the left side to move through the shot first, which results in staying behind the ball.

2. HIT DOWN AND THROUGH THE BALL

Here is another cliche to watch out for: Hit down and through the ball. It's true that the club goes down and through the ball if you make a good swing. But you can't just hit down on the ball in any old way and expect results. There is a sequence to it.

First, you set up with your hands ahead of the ball. Since you are moving your body toward the target as you swing, it makes sense that the hands will be ahead of the ball at impact. That is automatic. This means, then, that the path of the swing will be downward as you swing through the impact area. It will allow you to hit the ball first, then the turf, which is correct.

Golfers sometimes do not understand that this action is the result of a correct sequence of movements. There's no trick to hitting down on the ball, if that's what you want to do. But you want the ball to go a long way, not down into the ground. We want the ball to go out, and up!

3. SWING WITHIN YOURSELF

I think many golfers misinterpret the meaning of "swing within yourself." Swinging within yourself does not mean making half-shots. It means taking a full swing and using *much* of your power, but not *all* your power. It means swinging hard, but always with the idea of keeping your rhythm, balance, and timing. If you lose these things, then you are not swinging within yourself.

A famous golfer saying that she's swinging as hard as she can means that she is swinging as hard as she can while still retaining timing and balance. Personally, when I rare back, I know I am probably going to lose either or both. What I lose in control is far more critical than any distance I might gain. I believe that the single most critical error that causes badly hit shots is swinging outside oneself.

I play in a lot of Pro-Ams where I'm paired with amateurs, so I see a lot of different golf swings. There are many variations in these swings, but two elements are constants: One is the business of swinging too hard; the other is not using enough club on approach shots to the green. If I could play a single practice round with my amateur partners, with the idea of lowering their scores the following day, I would concentrate on those two areas.

4. KEEP YOUR HEAD DOWN

Keep your head down. You've heard it a thousand times. I suspect you've also found that it's virtually impossible to ''hold'' the head down and play consistently. That's because it is unnatural, with all the forces at work in the golf swing. Natural momentum makes the head want to move.

It's natural to keep the head still at impact and then let it come up easily to watch the flight of the shot. But if you're thinking about holding your head down, you're not thinking the right thought. Your real intent should be to keep your eye on the ball. The main reason for keeping your eye on the ball through impact is to enable you to see it! To do that, you must keep the head somewhat *steady*, which is quite different from holding the head *down*. It takes big muscles to hold the head in a still position. Unfortunately, those muscles are in the back and when you hold your head still, you are bunching up those muscles, tensing your body, and keeping it from making that smooth, coordinated effort that is a good golf swing. Rhythm and coordination are out the window.

Holding the head still after impact can also cause you to lose balance. If you step forward on your follow-through, that is often what has happened.

Ordinarily, we don't pay attention to what happens after impact because the ball is already on its way. However, what caused you to fall forward and lose your balance affects the flight of the ball. That cause took place somewhere in the downswing and probably had something to do with head position.

The entire head problem can be solved by being natural. Keep your head somewhat steady as you hit the ball simply because that's the only way you can get a good look at it. Then, at impact and as the weight shift is taking place, simply let the head come up so that you can follow the flight of the ball. Think of the natural momentum of the swing doing all the work for you.

5. DON'T REVERSE-PIVOT

Pivot is another term for weight shift, but it's not a term I like because it's difficult to understand. A reverse-pivot occurs when you incorrectly shift your weight. Instead of moving the weight to the right foot on the backswing, then back to the left side on the downswing, the golfer does just the opposite—shifting the weight to the left side on the backswing, then finishing the swing with the weight on the right foot.

To shift the weight correctly, start in the correct address position. This tip is simple but true. The fundamentals—grip, stance, and alignment—come first. The weight shift comes later. The weight shift is not a big, big move. It is a very subtle one and it happens in a small area, between the left and right feet.

The correct weight shift happens when you start the club back. As your torso turns away from the ball, the weight shifts across the inside of your left foot to your right foot. On the downswing, your weight should move back to the left side.

The weight shift to the left side should begin with a slight lateral move of the hips. In other words, on your backswing you make a hip turn and shoulder turn, but when you come back through you don't just turn out of the way or make an immediate turn to the left side. You drive into a more lateral move with your body, which throws the club into a downward path. This lateral move happens when the hips move slightly to the left on a line parallel with the line to the target, rather than spinning out of the way.

6. AT IMPACT, YOU SHOULD RETURN TO ADDRESS POSITION

Wrong. You don't really return to the address position at impact because you are in motion. When you're in motion, your hips and hands are already past the ball when your club strikes it.

The weight shift on the downswing, the momentum of that shift to the left side with your hands still cocked and your body moving toward the target, helps create a good position at impact.

If you did return to the address position at impact, you would be in a stationary position—you would stop all your momentum toward the target. You might hit the ball, but you would not get much distance. "Let the ball get in the way of your swing," is a *better* cliche to help you make a correct swing.

7. SPEED UP YOUR HAND ACTION

What the heck is hand action? When you come through the ball, you don't have time to think, "Now I'll uncock my wrists." What you should be doing is allowing the club to take its natural course.

When you have a good grip and a proper turn and backswing,

and when you come through the shot by staying on the same level and moving your weight to the left side, then your hands will come through the shot correctly. That is, they will come through correctly unless you make some adjustment. Good hand action is the result of other fundamentals, but you don't consciously develop this. It just happens.

This is where a good teaching professional is helpful. I was taught that the proper hand action derives naturally from the forearms, which cause a rotation of the clubhead back to a square position at impact. The hands don't function independently in your swing; they are a part of the whole.

8. SLICERS SHOULD LINE UP TO THE LEFT OF THE TARGET

Most people who slice compensate by lining up more and more to the left of the target. As a result, they get a bigger slice because, subconsciously, they know they're lined up too far left. Their natural feel takes over and they automatically push the ball back to the right.

The reverse is also true for golfers who hook the ball and compensate by lining up to the right of the target. By doing that, they have to hook the ball more and more back to the target.

The best way to get rid of a slice is to first make sure that your grip and fundamentals are correct. Then, line up straight at the target and try to get your clubface square through the ball.

There are only two things that cause a ball to go to the right and two things that cause it to go to the left. The first is the path of the clubhead at impact. The second is the position of the clubface at impact. If you understand this, you'll have a better chance of developing a swing that will consistently hit the ball on line.

In a slice, the path of the clubhead is coming across the ball. If the clubface is square, the ball will go to the right. If the clubhead comes across the line and the clubface is closed, the shot will be pulled to the left. If the clubhead comes across the line and the face is open, the ball will be pushed to the right.

A hook is created when the path of the clubhead is coming in on a straight line and the clubface is closed. If the path of the clubhead comes across the ball from the inside, you'll get a big roundhouse hook.

To avoid these problems, first check your grip. Be sure that the blade is square, then take your grip. Then you'll know if your problem is caused by the path of the clubhead or an open clubface.

Another point to remember is that the more you line up to the right of the target, the more you will subconsciously close the face at address. The opposite is also true. The more you line up to the left of the target, the more you will subconsciously open the face at address. Both positions will get you into swing trouble. Practice lining up straight at the target with a square blade.

9. FINESSE THE SHOT

What is ''finesse''? Finesse occurs when you have a little leeway about how hard to hit a shot. In a bunker, the leeway involves how much sand to take. If you have finesse, you have some sort of feel about where you want to hit the ball and how far you want it to run.

Finesse really means just knowing, through practice, how far back and how far through to take the clubhead. Any time you're dealing with a less than full swing, it's called finesse, or feel. That's all it is. You have to practice these less-than-full shots in order to determine how *hard* to hit the ball.

10. THE WIND DOESN'T AFFECT A WELL-STRUCK BALL

This is basically true because of the spin of the ball. Another cliche is that a straight shot is a mistake. That's also true.

Usually, when a ball is well hit, the club puts a slight spin on the ball. The spin on the ball affects the path of the ball. Some professionals fade the ball, some draw their shots. I draw the ball. The draw is the *result* of hitting the ball correctly with the club coming into the ball on the proper path, and the ball falling to the left in its flight pattern.

The wind will affect a draw to some degree, but not very much, especially if the wind is blowing strongly left to right. The same applies with a fade in a right-to-left wind. If you put spin on the ball, and nearly all of us do, the ball *will* be more affected by a crosswind blowing in the same direction as the ball is moving. A strong wind in your face will especially affect high shots, and a backwind may cause you to overshoot your target.

The simpler you can make your golf swing, the better you will play, and although that in itself sounds somewhat like a cliche, it shouldn't be taken that way. What I'm trying to give you is an understanding for evaluating cliches. Once you have that understanding, then when a seemingly profound cliche comes along, you can listen; but if it doesn't agree with your knowledge, you can discard it before it causes you to develop a swing problem.

Trouble Shots

Trouble lurks everywhere on a golf course. Most fairways are marred by divots, and lined with trees and high rough. Bunkers block your shots to the green and the wind blows your ball off line.

After you have reached a certain stage of proficiency in your game, you will begin to recognize situations where it would be better to hit shots with something other than a normal swing. The most common problem you'll encounter on the golf course, other than bunker shots (see "Taking the Fear out of Bunker Shots"), will be high rough.

PLAYING FROM HIGH ROUGH

Certain clubs are designed specifically for playing out of high rough. As you become more advanced, you'll want to add these to your bag. Both the 5-wood and 6-wood work well out of the rough. Other woods designed for play from the rough have brand names, like the Baffler, Ginty, and the Rough-Rider. They all work.

It's better to use a wood, rather than an iron, out of the rough, where the longer grass tends to grab the clubhead of an iron. So I always recommend using a wood, especially for women. Even if the shot out of the rough is not a long one, you can always grip down on the wood and hit it a shorter distance.

The shot from high rough is difficult to play. Bermuda grass is probably the worst because the grass blades are tough, yet the ball sinks down among them. One way to play this shot is to open the clubface slightly, then take your grip. You'll need such a clubface because the high grass will cause the clubface to close as you strike the ball, the club will tend to turn in your hand, and the shot will tend to go to the left.

90

Always make a conscious effort to grip the club very firmly with your left hand when you are hitting from high rough. This will help you to keep the clubface square through the shot and prevent the blade from closing.

When you swing, don't try to contact the ball first. If you attempt to have a more vertical downswing in order to contact the ball first, your club will grab so much grass going through the shot that you'll never get out!

All you want to do on this shot is to get the clubface moving level with the ball at impact. This is more of a sweeping shot than a downward blow.

HITTING FROM A DIVOT

Occasionally, your ball will land right in the middle of the fairway but you'll be dismayed to discover that the ball is sitting in a divot, or perhaps a slight indentation in the ground. This is just bad luck, but there's a way to hit a decent shot out of such a poor lie.

Unless the divot is an awfully deep one, hitting out of a divot is not as scary as you might think. Many golfers open the blade of the club and try to cut the ball out of a divot. That's probably the worst thing you can do, unless you are extremely strong. The easiest way to hit the ball from a divot is to close your clubface.

The 5-wood is a great club for this. To play the shot, close the clubface slightly, then take your grip. Play the ball somewhat back in your stance, in other words, right of center, because you want to catch the ball on your downswing with a descending blow.

You want to contact the ball first, turf afterward, with a more vertical downswing than usual. You want the clubface coming at the ball as if it were driving the ball into the ground. The reason for this is that the ground actually helps you by pinching the club and ball together as they meet. The ball then travels up the face of the club and comes out easily.

If you try to play a cut shot with an open clubface, the bottom part of the blade, rather than the clubface, comes down on the ball. That's why I close the face slightly. Because the face is closed, you must allow for a slight hook (the shot will have a low trajectory), and the ball will run quite a bit when it lands. Allow for this when you line up and take your stance. This is not going to be a great-looking shot, but it will come out.

LOW SHOTS

To hit a low golf shot, use a lower take-away than on a normal shot. Usually, you take the clubhead back low for about one foot on your backswing. To hit a low shot, extend that low take-away a little.

Most likely you're only going to take a ¾ swing with this shot and the lower take-away helps you extend your arc so that you can still generate power. This lower extension is done mostly with your arms. Play the ball back of center in your stance.

Club selection is critical to this shot. There is almost no way you can hit an intentionally low 7-, 8-, or 9-iron. I seldom attempt to hit a low shot with any club more lofted than a 5-iron. If you don't have far to go, just grip down on the club.

When you come through the shot, instead of letting the club pull you through and up into your finish, extend the club a bit lower on your follow-through. That's the purpose of playing the ball back in your stance, because you'll have a better chance of keeping the club low as you go through the ball. This gives the ball a lower trajectory from the moment of impact.

On this shot, especially with longer clubs, you'll have a tendency to draw the ball, simply because the ball is back of center and the clubface comes into it slightly closed. Experiment on the practice tee to learn how much you draw the ball, then adjust for it when you play this shot on the course.

Use a ¾ swing because the combination of the back-of-center ball position and the lower, longer take-away will restrict your ability to make a full turn.

It's also possible to hit a low shot just by making sure your hands are ahead of the ball at impact, but this is a very difficult shot. It's much easier to play the ball back in your stance.

Low shots are usually necessary when you're hitting into the wind. If you would hit a 6-iron on a calm day, take a 5-iron and hit it low to keep it under the wind. The wind will hold it up and cause the ball to bite. If you play a low shot without wind to hold it up, the ball will roll more when it hits, so you must allow for added roll.

The biggest mistake made by golfers I see occurs when they're close to a green with a bunker in front of them and they have to go under a tree limb. There's no way to loft the ball over the bunker, miss the limb, and hold the green. It's an almost impossible shot. Instead, play the percentages. Play to one side of the bunker with a low shot to get on the green.

HIGH SHOTS

Execution of a high shot is the opposite of the low shot. Play the ball forward of center in your stance. Again, choice of clubs is important. It's difficult to get the ball up high into the air with anything less lofted than a 3-iron.

The swing is normal, except that you should concentrate on a high finish, which will help lift the ball as you come through the impact area.

Although you use a low take-away for a low shot, the opposite doesn't apply to a high shot. The take-away is normal.

You can open the blade slightly, which automatically sets you up for a fade. Again, experiment with different clubs to see how much fade each club produces. A good rule is that the longer the club, the more you'll bend the ball. It's also difficult to fade the ball much with a short iron.

For a very high shot, such as the kind you need to hit over a tree, some pros recommend that you pick up the club quickly on your backswing. I don't agree. I play the ball slightly forward in my stance, open the blade, take a normal swing, and try to swing to the trajectory I want the ball to take. In other words, I'll try to swing to the top of the tree.

At alignment, look up to the top of the tree and get that point in your mind. Keep it in mind as you swing and swing the club up to it. The ball will come up more quickly than normal. This is called visualization and it works on high and low shots.

Knowing how the ball will react is one of the fun things about trouble shots. There's nothing that gives me greater pleasure than making a good trouble shot. In fact, I think trouble shots are my strong point and I take a great deal of pride in being able to make them a large percentage of the time.

INTENTIONAL DRAW

Mickey Wright gave me the best tip on the intentional draw. She said to do everything as you usually would, but come into the ball with the face slightly closed, and the ball will draw. That's true.

There is one catch, but it's easily overcome. What you should do is close the clubface slightly at address, *then take your grip*. Most players do just the opposite. Then, when they swing, their hands come into the ball in a normal way, as does the clubhead, and there's no draw.

Once you understand that all-important point about the grip, there's nothing to making this shot. This is the simplest technique for the draw. I do this when I want to hit a big hook, slowing the swing through the hitting area. That lets the clubhead pass the hands, and the face is really hooded.

INTENTIONAL FADE

To fade the ball, take your grip with the clubface slightly open. A slice will result if you speed your swing through the impact area because the clubface will stay severely open and create a bigger bend.

With either the draw or the fade, you need to make the necessary adjustments in your alignment.

I have one concern on these trouble shots. Unless you have been playing golf for quite awhile, these shots may be something that you do not yet have the ability to do. My goal in this book is to help you play better and to enjoy the game. If you try something of which you are not as yet capable, it may hinder your enjoyment, so wait until your game is ready before you try these finer points.

You'll have the best opportunity to learn these shots if you try to understand the position of the clubface needed to produce them. There is only one thing that will cause a ball to turn left, and that is a closed clubface. The opposite is true for the ball turning right.

I always close my golf clinics by saying, "See your pro." Learning golf is one thing you cannot do by yourself. The pro can see what you're doing. A pro can then be of much greater help than a system of trial and error.

TROUBLE SHOT CHECKLIST

- High rough: Open the clubface slightly. Grip the club firmly, especially with the left hand. Make a sweeping downswing rather than a vertical one, and just hang on!
- From a divot: Line up allowing for a low, running shot, which will move right to left. Close the clubface slightly before you take your grip. Play the ball back in your stance. Hit the ball first, turf afterward, with a descending blow.
- Low shots: Line up allowing for the ball to move very slightly right-to-left. Use a less-lofted club. Play the ball back of center in your stance. Make a long, low take-away and a low follow-through. Use a ¾ backswing and a ¾ follow-through.
- High shots: Line up allowing for a slight left-to-right movement of the shot. Play the ball forward of center in your stance. Pick up the club slightly on your backswing. Concentrate on a high finish.
- Intentional draw: Close the clubface slightly, then take your grip. Make a normal swing. For a bigger hook, slow the swing through the hitting area.
- Intentional fade: Open the clubface slightly, then take your grip. Make a normal swing. For a bigger slice, speed up your swing through the impact area.

Sneaky Trouble Shots

Some trouble shots are so innocent looking that we don't realize we're in trouble! I'm not referring to the obvious, like shots out of trees or bunkers. These problems are more subtle. It's my opinion that 40 to 50 percent of all golf shots have a touch of trouble connected with them, and we never know it.

If you recognize them, you'll avoid a lot of mis-hits. Many shots that end up right or left of where you've aimed, or short or long of the target, will be eliminated. You can outwit trouble before you get into it.

Two of the biggest factors are the lie of the ball in the fairway and the terrain. On every shot I play, on my way to the ball my first thought is whether or not there is any element of trouble in the upcoming shot, even if I'm in the dead center of the fairway.

To avoid trouble you must evaluate how well or poorly the ball is sitting up on the grass, whether your feet are above or below the ball, and if there is a slight hill where the ball sits. Often, we completely overlook these potential problems and just swing. That's when we lose the ball left or right or hit fat shots or blade the ball.

You can eliminate those bad shots with just a little forethought.

PLAYING A BALL BELOW YOUR FEET

Here's an example: Suppose the ball is slightly below your feet. Since you will not be able to get the full force of your swing behind the shot, take a slightly longer club, which will deliver the extra force you need.

When the ball is below your feet, flex your knees to bring yourself closer to the ball. This will help you keep your weight more on the heels.

Since the ball is below your feet, it's a little farther away from you. You'll also have a problem with balance, so you won't be able to put as much force into the shot. A slightly longer club will equal out the distance.

Bend from the knees to bring yourself closer to the ball and, for improved balance, keep your weight more on your heels throughout the swing. This shot will move left to right, so allow for that when you line up.

It's a good idea to try a few shots like this on the practice tee. Just find a slight slope and hit a few balls from it.

PLAYING A BALL ABOVE YOUR FEET

Having the ball above your feet is the opposite of its being below. Almost automatically you will draw or hook this shot, so you must

When the ball is above your feet, stand more erect, use a shorter club, and allow for a hook.

When the ball is above your feet, you'll have a tendency to fall away from the ball when you swing, so work hard on maintaining your balance.

take that into account. Also, on this shot, your swing plane is going to be a little flatter. You might need to take a shorter club because the ball is closer to you.

When the ball is above your feet, you'll have a tendency to fall away from the ball so you must try very hard to keep your balance.

UPHILL AND DOWNHILL LIES

When you find yourself with an uphill or downhill lie, when one foot is higher than the other, you have two areas of adjustment. Only one is really critical: With one leg bent more than the other to accommodate the hill, as you settle into a comfortable address position, align your shoulders parallel with the horizon. You need to work at that. It does not come naturally.

Let's say you have a downhill lie, which means your right foot will be higher than your left. You won't feel comfortable at address unless your right leg is bent more than your left leg. There is a natural tendency for your shoulders to slant down the hill. The trick is to get your shoulders parallel with the horizon. This is important.

For an uphill or a downhill lie, the shoulders and hips should be parallel with the horizon—completely level, despite the slope of the terrain.

If you don't do it, you will not be able to make a normal swing at the ball.

On a downhill lie, you should play the ball a little farther back in your stance, so you might choose a slightly more lofted club. Since the club will come into the ball more quickly, this extra loft will be of help because you'll have a tendency to get more distance with this shot. To be specific, if you are in 6-iron territory, use a

Although I have a downhill lie, I've leveled my hips and shoulders, which will enable me to make a proper swing.

7-iron instead. Also, you will normally have trouble getting a shot from this lie into the air, and the extra loft will help.

The opposite trouble is the uphill lie. The same thinking applies, but in reverse. The ball is played more toward the uphill foot. The left leg is bent to accommodate the hill, and the shoulders are

Facing a downhill lie, I have bent my right leg to accommodate the hill, and my hips and shoulders are level with the horizon.

arranged parallel with the horizon. You might use one club stronger than you would use from a level lie, because the uphill angle will make the ball go higher than you expected, which will also decrease distance. A lower-lofted club will help you. For instance, if you're in 6-iron territory on an uphill lie, you might use a 5-iron instead.

Facing an uphill lie, I have bent my left leg to accommodate the hill. This puts my hips and shoulders level with the horizon.

The proper address position, shown at the beginning of the sequence on the opposite page, will help you make a good fundamental swing, no matter how difficult the lie.

THE SHOT TO THE GREEN

The greens, by themselves, should be thought of as a specific form of trouble because the green dictates shot execution if you're trying to get close to the flagstick.

On greens that are difficult to hold, you obviously need to play as much of a lofted club as you can in order to stop the ball quickly. This is not always possible, and you may elect to run the ball onto the green in an effort to stop it near the hole. If there is nothing in front of the green, like a slope that would make the ball do funny things, then the pitch-and-run is the best shot to play.

Another difficult green is the elevated green that is flat on top. Here you need to hit the highest possible shot and hope that it will land softly. This is a difficult shot, even if you are hitting to the green from the fairway, so you need a special plan.

The problem with this kind of shot is that it is going to land a lot quicker than a normal shot with the same club, and consequently will not bite as well. You need to get the shot up as high as you can in order to get the most bite on it. The greater backspin causes the ball to stop quickly.

Let's say you have an 8-iron. You might be better off using a 7-iron and trying to hit it very high, which will take some distance off the club. You do that by playing the ball a bit forward in your stance. You might also open the blade very slightly. Be sure to finish with a high follow-through.

These may be trouble shots but I think you will find the game a lot more fun once you begin to zero in on these seemingly innocent shots, have a plan, and try to execute it. This is when you really begin to learn to play *golf!*

SNEAKY TROUBLE SHOT CHECKLIST

- Ball below feet: Use a slightly longer club. Allow for a left-to-right shot. Concentrate on balance.
- Ball above feet: Use a shorter club. Allow for a right-to-left shot. Concentrate on balance.
- Downhill lie: Align shoulders parallel to horizon. Play ball back of center. Use a more lofted club.
- Uphill lie: Align shoulders parallel to horizon. Play ball forward of center. Use a less lofted club.
- Shot to slick greens: Use a very lofted club or consider playing a pitch-and-run.
- Elevated greens: Use a less lofted club but hit it high. Open blade slightly. Play ball left of center. Finish high.

Playing in Bad Weather

Playing in bad weather, such as in wind or rain, is difficult.

Playing conditions are such that you are unable to play well enough to shoot a great score. It's just going to be tough and you can't fight it. The weather will affect the ball, will make some holes play really long, and make a hard hole even more difficult. Sometimes, in bad weather, bogey is not a bad round.

In the wind, control is more important than ever. You don't want to take a wild swing, because that will probably put additional spin on the ball, allowing the wind to take the ball and make a wild shot even worse. For instance, if you're playing in a right-to-left wind, and you make a really big swing and hit a huge draw, the wind will take it farther left.

There's an old saying that the wind will not affect a well-struck ball. Well, that's true, but only to a point. The reason the wind doesn't move a ball that has been hit well is that the ball has no great amount of spin on it, just a little spin. But if you really hook or really slice a shot, the wind compounds the error.

You are looking for control.

Patty Berg coined the phrase, "When it's breezy, swing easy." That's a very good thing to remember. Unfortunately, when we are playing in the wind, we usually *want* to hit it harder, but that's incorrect.

PLAYING INTO THE WIND

Into the wind, take your usual swing but accept the fact that you're not going to hit the ball as far as you usually do because the wind will not allow it. Do not try to hit it harder. Try to hit the ball as well as you can into the wind, and still have control over it.

When I play, I sometimes feel that the wind can knock me off balance and, unfortunately, my swing gets a lot shorter because of that. But I don't try to hit the ball very hard. I try to *bump* the ball; I take a shorter, easier swing and I use more club for the shot than I usually would.

Of course, it's much easier to get the ball high into the wind because the wind's resistance makes the ball climb. It's not so much that you, the player, are hitting the ball high. It is the wind picking up the ball and putting it into the air and carrying it upward.

PLAYING DOWNWIND

Downwind shots are difficult too. It's very hard to get the ball up in the air going downwind because you must cut through the wind to get the shot up. The ball will go farther without the player having to ''lift'' the ball into the air, but it's not going to carry that much farther.

The reason it won't carry is that, downwind, you're trying to get the ball up into the air quickly. To do that you use a lot of force just trying to get the ball airborne. So, don't try to do anything more than use your normal swing force and the ball will get up.

If you are playing downwind and need extra carry on a shot that would normally require a 6-iron, you might choose a 7-iron instead. It's much easier to get the ball up with a more lofted club, and it doesn't require much effort to hit a downwind 7-iron as far as a normal 6-iron.

Downwind, you must also judge how far the ball is going to carry, but that really depends upon how hard the wind is blowing. Downwind shots are made even harder because you cannot stop the ball.

Sometimes the wind is gusty. This is the most difficult of wind conditions because the wind swirls.

Here's something to remember. If you're trying to carry over water downwind, the worst thing you can do is not carry the water. If you go in, you'll automatically pick up a penalty stroke. However, because you're using a club strong enough to carry the water, and because you're downwind (which takes backspin off of the shot), your shot may not hold the green either.

I always favor playing the percentages. If the trouble is in front of the green, you must carry over it. If the trouble is in back of the green, you've got to make sure you don't hit your ball over the green.

CLUB SELECTION

Club selection is especially crucial in windy conditions.

Even when I'm going downwind, I don't take a big swing. You have to have better balance and that's why you need to swing a little easier.

A crosswind knocks the ball down too. Any time you think a ball will travel in a direction other than a straight line, you need to take a stronger club. Any time you plan to fade or hook the ball—even though a hook will *roll* farther—as far as carry is concerned, you've got to take a stronger club.

Again, control is crucial.

Here's some advice for the low handicap player. If it's a right-to-left wind, I feel I have more control if I fade or "cut" the ball into the wind. Because I'm putting a left-to-right spin on the ball, the wind will hold the ball up and the shot should go pretty close to where I want it to go.

If I hit a draw—a right-to-left shot into a right-to-left wind—the shot becomes too complicated. I must ask myself how much farther to the right I have to play. How much do I hook it? How far will it roll? I just don't feel that I have that much control with a hook in a right-to-left wind. But in a left-to-right wind, I try to hold the shot back into the wind with a slight draw.

Sometimes I may not want to play any kind of fade or hook. I may want to play a shot that I can just throw up into the air and let the wind take it.

PLAYING IN THE RAIN

Rain is just messy. It's very easy to hit the ball "fat" in wet weather. This often happens because the ball sits down in the wet grass; meanwhile, your feet are slipping, and there's a tendency to hit behind the ball.

In dry weather we are sometimes not even aware that we occasionally hit the ground and the ball at the same moment. We get away with it. But on a wet day, with the ball sitting down, the wet grass grabs the clubhead and makes it harder to get through the shot. Be aware of this tendency in wet weather.

I guard against a fat shot by playing the ball back a little in my stance. I also try to hit the ball with more of a descending blow because I am trying to dig it out of wet grass.

On a rainy day the air is also heavier than normal, so you need to use more club than you usually would.

The main thing to remember is to keep your grips dry. If the equipment gets wet, you might as well call it a day. If you think it's going to rain, try to carry an extra towel and an extra glove, use your umbrella, and be sure you cover your clubs.

Be sure to dry your clubshaft, as well as the clubhead, or the water will run down onto the grip when you put the club into the bag.

Rain even changes putting. Putts will not break as much on a wet green because you must strike the putt so hard to get it to the hole. However, this depends upon *where* the break is. If the break comes late in the putt, when the ball is close to the hole, when the ball begins to slow down it may still break. If the break is at the front of the putt, close to its origin, it probably will not break at all because you have had to hit the putt so hard.

These are conditions to keep in mind when playing in the rain: The greens will be slower. The fairways will be slower and you won't get as much roll, so the course will play a lot longer. And, unfortunately, your round will take more time. It's just going to be a messy day, and you'll play a lot better if you just accept that.

WIND AND RAIN CHECKLIST

- When it's breezy, swing easy.
- Use a shorter, easier swing into the wind and use more club.
- Use an easier swing, downwind, and less club.
- On wet grass, play ball back of center; use a descending blow.
- Use more club on wet days.
- Keep your grips and clubshafts dry.
- Allow for slower greens and less break on putts.

How to Play "Thinking" Golf

There's a lot to consider when playing a golf shot: the lie, whether the ball is sitting up or down, whether it's on soft ground or hardpan. This is when you really begin to be a player. If you are thinking of your swing on the golf course, you have no chance. You cannot be working on your golf swing because if you are, you're not thinking about what you're trying to do, which is to get the ball into the hole.

When the pressure is on, when you have to make a shot, your concentration needs to be on your purpose, which is to score and to get the ball into the hole in as few strokes as possible.

You cannot be trying to hit the perfect shot or make the perfect swing. For instance, if you have a perfect putting stroke but you are lined up to the right or left, or hit the putt too softly, the perfection of the stroke does not matter. You must concentrate on what you are trying to do and where you are trying to go. That's when you learn how to play the golf course.

I learned this on the tour years ago. In 1962 I became too swing conscious. I could hardly get the club back during a round. I had forgotten what I was trying to do, which was to get the ball around. I didn't trust my swing. It's one thing to stand on the practice tee and hit ball after ball, but if you're not concentrating on where you are hitting the ball and how you are getting it there, it's very difficult to take that swing to the golf course.

Because I was having such problems, I talked to Mickey Wright. I said, "I practice all the time, but when I get to the golf course I cannot hit it a lick. I practically fan it and I'm freezing over the ball. I have no idea of what I'm doing. Is there such a thing as being too swing conscious?" She assured me that there was.

Coming from Mickey, that was a big deal, so from that day on I stopped thinking of the swing when I played. I just stood up and hit the ball.

I let my natural feel take over and trusted my swing. If I hit it into the boonies, I'd just go find it and try to hit it again. That's scary, but the other way wasn't working. That's when I began to learn to play the courses, and the strategy of how best to play a hole because I made myself forget the mechanics of the swing. You can't *try* to make a perfect swing because you get so frozen that you have no feel. You must put your mind to your target, and that's where you build confidence in your own ability. I learned that my swing may not look very pretty, but I knew where the ball was going. That was a great feeling. It was like being let out of jail—freedom.

The key is not to panic if you hit the ball into trouble. I hit it into a lot of trouble, but I was not afraid of hitting it off line. If I did, I'd just try to hit it back to the fairway. If you are worried about *why* you hit it over here, you are thinking behind instead of forward. You must think forward. That's why people say you must forget the last hole.

One of the nicest compliments Mickey ever gave me was when she said, "You adjust better than anyone I ever saw." If I'm hooking or slicing very badly, or doing something really terrible on the golf course, I just play it until I get in. Then I work on the swing to try to get out of it before the next round. My attitude always was, "Well, there's nothing I can do about it now. I'll go with what I've got and work it out later." I never stop striving for a better swing. I don't think that you ever do. You go through times when you think, "Oh boy, I've got it now," and that's when you get a streak of good playing. There are good streaks and bad streaks. A good streak usually happens when you are concentrating well. That's when you win three and four tournaments in a row. It's wonderful!

You never stop learning about the swing. You can't really teach feel because feel is developed. People say, "I felt like this when I hit the ball well." They are always trying to re-create that shot or that feel. When you are hitting the ball well, you did something fundamentally correct. That's what created that feel for you. So, you should concentrate on the fundamentals and that feel will come back.

However, feel changes from day to day. People worry about their swings, but their swings do not change overnight; feel does. That's why golf is such a terrifically hard game. Some days you wake up feeling just great, and some days you don't.

Timing has a lot to do with it. Some days you're calm and your timing is good.

Sometimes I've heard players come in after a great round and say, "I felt like I was in a fog all day." Sometimes players who are ill will have a great round. It's because their illness has taken their mind off of everything but each shot. They're just trying to get in. They just play. If they hit a bad shot they don't worry about it, they just hit the next shot.

There are people who play consistently well, day in and day out, like Tom Kite. Tom is consistently near the top ten. He is in control of what he is doing. His timing and feel change, but his swing is in control and he knows what he is doing. He can adjust. He's not trying to hit the ball in the same spot every day.

Louise Suggs, Patty Berg, and Mickey Wright were terribly consistent. It looked as if they hit the ball the same way every time, as if they never missed a shot. Of course, they did hit the ball into trouble sometimes, but they knew how to get it out of trouble. They were in control of what they were doing and they were concentrating on what they were doing. They never let the troublesome shot disturb them enough that they could not play the next shot. They were marvelous to watch.

It's great to watch somebody dissect a golf course. Ben Hogan was always accused of replacing his divot. He was so consistent in the way that he struck the ball that he knew he was going to hit it to that same spot the next day. That's why Hogan was so great, that's why Byron Nelson was so great, that's why Jack Nicklaus is so great.

Nicklaus's concentration is revered. He is really into what he is doing and you can see that in the way that he stares at the ball. I'm sure Jack doesn't realize he is staring, he is just concentrating so hard on what he is doing. He's in control of himself and his game. That's not something you're born with. It's something you must work on and develop.

Some people believe you only have to concentrate a few seconds on each shot. That's true for some people; I believe Mickey plays this way. But if I let myself wander too far, and not keep myself involved in what I'm trying to do, I don't believe I can pull my concentration back in that quickly in just a few seconds.

It's work. It's hard work to concentrate and it can just wear you out, but this is an important part of playing the game well. Thinking your way around the golf course is just as important as swinging the club.

More Golf Course
Strategy

What I admire most about women amateur golfers is their great ability to switch gears. They have so many things going, so many distractions, and yet most manage to play quite well.

Most women golfers don't think about what they're going to do when they get to the golf course. Most of you have so many things on your mind: what to cook for dinner, when to pick up the kids, the house needs cleaning, there's this chore or that. Facing those pressures, it's remarkable that you even make your tee time. Most women I know dash to the course, jump out of the car, throw on their shoes, and play.

Because of these intrusions, women seldom take time to practice or to develop a golf swing. One way to enjoy the game more and score better is by thinking about playing the golf course rather than getting upset about bad shots.

We all hit bad shots, but it's better to just keep thinking forward. Try saying to yourself, "Okay, I goofed that shot, but what's the best way for me to get to the green in fewer strokes." That was one of the hardest things I ever had to learn in golf. It's still a very difficult thing for me to do. Concentrating on the shot at hand is an act of blotting out what is behind you. I'm referring to your way of thinking on the golf course. Of course, a bad shot is still possible even though you're thinking well. If I hit a bad shot, I simply walk to it as calmly as I can and play the percentages on the next shot. Then, I'm at least assured of getting the ball back into play. It works! By doing that, I redirect my thinking into constructive channels and, surprisingly, I find my game improving. After a bad shot, although I am playing for bogey, I no longer worry about it because I know my focus is in the right place. The next tee becomes a fresh opportunity, something to look forward to.

Golf is a game of misses, and the winners are those who have the best misses. When I first came out on the tour, I watched players like Patty Berg and Mickey Wright with wonder. If they were playing poorly, their scores were often as low as my good rounds. If they played well, their scores were, of course, sensational. A bad round for them was seldom more than seventy-five. When playing in a fifty-four-hole or seventy-two-hole event, one round of seventy-five does not take you out of the running.

I played many rounds with Mickey. That meant that I had at least a few opportunities to watch her when she wasn't hitting the ball up to her own usual high standards. I marveled at the way she managed to score, in spite of these rare misses. I came to realize that it was her way of thinking on the golf course that helped her score. She was thinking well, regardless of how she was hitting the ball, and the results were there. *It is not essential to hit every shot perfectly to still be a winner*.

Once you realize that, you've taken the first major step toward salvaging a round of golf. It's also, in my opinion, the first major step toward playing better golf overall.

Course strategy is an important part of good thinking on the golf course. In good golf-course strategy, the obvious solution is not always the best solution.

If you're not a good bunker player, sometimes you might consider playing to the right of a bunker, rather than trying to go over it. Most women fear a bunker; those of you who do, please read the chapter "Taking the Fear out of Bunker Shots."

You might approach water hazards in the same way. You may consider wasting a shot and going around the hazard, rather than taking the risk of knocking your ball into the water. Average players take more risks than they are capable of dealing with. You need to evaluate your capabilities.

COURSE STRATEGY

Each golf course and each golf hole has its own characteristics.

Years ago this was even more apparent. Fairways and rough were not watered by sprinklers—only by rainfall—and they were much more firm.

In those days, if a fairway sloped from left to right, you'd try to either hook the ball back into the side of the hill, or start the ball over the left rough and play a fade, a shot that drops softly from left to right, because the ball would kick hard right.

Today we have watered fairways and watered rough and golf course conditioning has changed a great deal. On most courses you can probably hit the ball right at the middle of the fairway and it won't kick into the rough because the fairway is softer. However, you still need to plan your round by thinking about the characteristics of a hole.

It helps your concentration to play the golf course this way. You have a better chance of playing more consistent golf. Concentration is always very difficult, anyway. Using good course strategy not only helps you in tournament golf, it's more fun. It's fun because you are tested and asked to play different types of shots.

It also makes a player better appreciate the golf course she is playing. You see the course in a different light, rather than just going out and playing. Most players don't even look at a golf course in this way.

Thinking about course strategy puts a player in tune with the course. For example, if you are playing in a tournament or ladies day event, you'll be able to more quickly assess the danger if you're playing a new golf course. You can look at the terrain, you can look at the trouble, and know when you need to be careful. Maybe this sounds like a subtle approach, but it can make a difference in how you play your shot. There are times when you may not want to play for the center of the fairway, for instance, and you may need to play to the left side of a fairway.

The most important strategy is to look at a golf course hole by hole. When I play, I look at each hole and try to decide certain things: Is it straight away? Is it a dogleg hole? (A dogleg is a fairway that bends at an angle, either to the right or to the left; in other words, it's a bit crooked, like a dog's leg.) Can I cut across the corner of the dogleg? Do I need to stay left-center? How long is the dogleg? Can I fade the ball or hook the ball around the corner of the dogleg, or is the dogleg too long?

Some doglegs are short, and you really have to bend the shot or hit a shorter club, say a 3-wood or 2-iron, from the tee. If it's a long dogleg you don't have to worry about it. Just hit it straight and hope you can hit the ball to where the fairway bends.

ASSESSING THE TROUBLE

Before you play a hole, it's important to locate the trouble spots. Nine times out of ten, you will not hit the ball perfectly anyway. So, if you miss a shot, you want to try to miss it to a spot from which you have a recovery. I think the average player can reduce a number of strokes if she anticipates problems.

We all know there are certain places where you have a better chance of getting the ball out of trouble on one side rather than the other. Frequently you hear television commentators say, "The one place they don't want to miss it is over here because they have no recovery."

When pros hit a shot into a place from which they have no recovery, they say, "I've hit it in jail." All golfers want to avoid being "in jail" and need to take certain golf course subtleties into account.

When you are approaching a green, perhaps all the trouble is in front. So, you might take one more club than you normally would to be sure that you hit over that trouble. You have a better recovery from the back of the green than you do from the front of the green, for instance, so you want to be a little long.

If there's a lot of trouble in the back, maybe you don't want to be that aggressive on the hole. You would make sure you stay short instead of going over the green. That type of thinking can save players a lot of strokes.

Good golf course strategy helped me win the Dinah Shore Championship in 1977. The 18th hole at Mission Hills Country Club is a par 5 with water to the left of the tee-shot landing area. Before the final round, I had already decided how I was going to play that hole if I led the tournament.

The one place I did not want to lose it, of course, was to the left. So I made sure that I didn't. When I addressed my tee shot I lined up a little to the right side of the fairway. I knew my ball would probably bounce into the right rough but I knew that I could get a par from there. The one thing I didn't want to do was beat myself, which I would do if I tried to play a very hard, driving shot and tried to keep the ball in the fairway. That type of plan would bring the water into play.

I took the water out of play by blocking out the shot (keeping my left side very, very firm through the ball so that I could only miss the landing area to the right), and making sure that I hit my tee shot to the right. I played into the rough deliberately, but I had a good lie and could hit a fairway wood out of the rough. In the right rough I could have had two problems: I might have had a problem with trees and I might have had a bad lie. But neither problem was crucial nor would either cost a penalty stroke. I had to run that risk.

However, if I hit it into the water, I had no chance because I would have been penalized one stroke. I would have beaten myself. If I hit the ball to the right, I was at least dry and could hit it again.

I would at least be able to salvage a par on that final hole.

Happily, I hit a good shot back to the fairway and I was able to hit a short iron onto the green and two-putt for a par. That win remains one of my favorites.

Ironically, before I played the hole I thought I had a two-shot lead. As it turned out, I only had a one-shot lead because JoAnne Carner had birdied the 18th hole to pull within one stroke. Had I known that, I still would have guarded against the water, because if I'd hit into the water I would have had to take a penalty stroke.

I wasn't going to beat myself by trying to hit it into the fairway. Why put on that extra pressure? Why not hit the ball into the rough? Who cares? I wasn't trying to prove anything to anybody. I was just trying to win.

One key to my game over the years is that I have never really cared how a shot looks, or whether people think I have played a hole correctly. I play the shots and the holes according to my own plan and count on the total score as a measure of how I played that day.

I'm a percentage player. The only way you can play the percentages is to know the golf course, know your ability, and know what is your best shot. Don't try to get fancy or do something you're not capable of doing.

Harvey Penick always said, "Don't play any shot you haven't practiced, unless you're just forced to." Why try to play a risky shot that you've never even tried?

ANALYZING A GOLF COURSE

A player must determine the best way she can play a golf hole, not the best way someone else might play it. Some players normally play a draw, a shot that moves slightly from right to left. Others normally hit a fade, which moves slightly left to right. All players must take their own way of striking the ball into account.

If a player thinks about how to best play the hole and keeps herself in position, her thinking process is correct. You can't always succeed, but if you keep thinking in that way, your chances are a lot better than if you aren't thinking at all!

There is a lot to think about when you're hitting to a green or putting. If you're in position to hit into the green, you look at which way the green slopes. The natural terrain is really the best guide. Look at the natural terrain around you. There's always a low point somewhere. If you can find it, that will help. Usually it's a natural pond or a hollow of some sort.

Of course, if the terrain is flat you don't have to worry. I grew up in flat country. That background actually helped my game because I had to really study hilly courses. Each time I played a hilly course I had to think about how to play it because I'd never played that type of course before.

So, you look for a low or high point on a course. Is the high point more visible, or the low point? When playing in Palm Springs, the television commentators always say that the putts break to the town of Indio. The putts break to Indio because we are playing in the foothills and Indio is the low point; it's not that Indio is some giant magnet. Even though the contour of the green slopes in another direction, the natural terrain, the natural gravity, keeps it from breaking as much because the gravity pulls it toward Indio.

NARROWING YOUR TARGET FOR BETTER SHOTS

The smaller your target, the straighter you are going to hit the ball. Frequently, people say that they hit the ball straighter when they play on tight courses with lots of trees. I think it's because they had to narrow their target. It's forced upon them.

One way to narrow your target is to *spot line*. Nicklaus does this on every shot. He picks out a single spot two or three feet ahead of his ball and in line with his target, and tries to line up to that spot. Nancy Lopez does it, as do many players. The idea is to pick a spot you think the ball should travel over to reach its preferred destination, and line up to that spot with the face of the club. That's narrowing your target. You can also line up at a pole or at a church steeple. Don't just look at the whole picture and think, gosh, I've got this huge fairway. When you do that, you're liable to hit it anywhere because you don't really have a target.

You often hear people say that you should hit to the fat (or largest area) of the green. I don't believe that. I think you have to target your shot and I always aim at the flagstick. But the key here is that, while I always aim at the flagstick, if I miss the shot I always make sure I miss it to the fat of the green. Or, if I miss the fairway or miss my target spot, I'm going to be sure that I miss it to the fat of the fairway, or to the side where I will have the best shot for my recovery.

Of course, with my own game I'm moving the ball, left to right, or right to left, playing the percentage shot. But I'm also aiming. I know that if I'm going to miss it, I'm going to make darn sure that I miss it to where I have a recovery. That doesn't always work, but that's the thought and that's what I'm trying to do.

Among all of the players I've known, I'd say the best at course strategy were Betsy Rawls, Patty Berg, and Louise Suggs.

Some of our younger players don't really understand course strategy. They see me hit here, then there, and they think I've missed it without seeing what I'm trying to do. This is a learning process and these are things that you learn, but you can't learn them unless you are looking for them.

It's true that you, the average player, may not be looking at the characteristics of a golf course because you're not in a tournament situation. You're just going out for fun. But sometimes the fun is to study the course. It can bring a whole other aspect of golf to the average player. It's just a habit you get into, but it's fun to do because you appreciate the course and the design of the hole. On occasion you may think the design is a bad one, but you may also appreciate the natural terrain.

Studying the course also helps you appreciate the great golf course architects, like A. W. Tillinghast. Tillinghast used the natural terrain well. Donald Ross is another great example. You hardly know a Donald Ross course until after you've played it. You like the course, you enjoy it, and so you ask who the designer was. When you find out it was Donald Ross, you think, no wonder I enjoyed it. Dick Wilson, the Fazio's, and Joe Lee also used natural terrain well. Their courses are always different because they are designed to fit the land, unlike designers whose courses are like rubber stamps of their previous work.

Some of our current architects build their courses to look alike. It doesn't matter where they are, in the mountains or the plains; their courses all look alike and you can tell immediately who designed them. But the golf courses of the great architects all look different, they fit the land they are built on. You may not be able to tell right away who designed the golf course, but you know you like it.

The course is what a professional is considering when she's playing. And if the average woman player considered the course in the same way, it might be more fun for her too. It's a different way of playing the game. It makes you more in tune with the golf course, assists your concentration, and might help you knock off a few strokes because of your new-found ability to anticipate trouble.

How to Practice

If you're a serious golfer and really want to become a much better player, the only way you're going to get there is through lessons and practice. Most golfers have very little time to practice, but it's amazing how practice sessions can improve a game.

Practicing can be a lot of fun. If you're only able to practice in your backyard, set up a small pitching target or use some of the many practice gadgets on the market, like a net and a practice mat to avoid digging up your lawn. This kind of practice can be very beneficial. Liselotte Neumann, who was on our LPGA Tour, grew up in Sweden where it was too cold to practice outdoors in the winter. In the cold months, Liselotte learned to swing by hitting balls into an indoor net and she became 1988 U.S. Women's Open Champion!

When you're a beginner, it's alright to just hit a lot of balls on the practice tee because all you're trying to do is learn to make contact and to build your confidence. As you become more confident, you might want to take a few lessons.

For more advanced golfers, even those just beyond the beginner stage, it's important to work on something concrete when you practice, rather than just hitting a lot of balls. Hitting balls without thinking about what you're doing will not help you anymore and may actually hurt you because you could be establishing a poor swing habit.

PRACTICE AS YOU PLAY

It's important to work on something positive, like alignment, ball position, address position, or your grip. Think about each shot as you hit it. It's not how many balls you hit that will improve the quality of your game. What *will* improve your game is practicing like you play and playing like you practice.

For example, when practicing, don't hit a lot of balls with one club. Start with a shorter iron, hit a couple of shots, then go to a medium iron, then to the driver, then back to the short iron, as if you are really playing on the golf course. Think about what you're doing as you hit these shots.

Harvey Penick oversaw hundreds of my practice sessions. I'd hit a few shots, then Harvey would say, "Now I'm going to visit with you a little." So I would stop hitting balls and chat with Harvey for a minute, then he would say, "Stand up there and hit that ball."

I really had to concentrate and rethink what I was doing after that short break but that's a good way to practice because golfers sometimes get into a rut hitting balls. They pound out ball after ball, without pause or thought. That's just wasted effort unless you're just trying to build up strength! I might mention here that hitting golf balls is the only way to really build the proper golf muscles, but hitting golf balls without thought will not help you improve your game.

A lot of golfers say, "Gee, I hit the ball well on the practice tee but I couldn't hit it at all on the golf course."

On the golf course you have no second chance. You have no second practice shot as you do on the driving range. On the golf course you feel tension and pressure because you suddenly care very much where the ball goes. Suddenly, the shots mean something. On the practice tee the shots mean nothing so, of course, you swing freely and smoothly. You're not really concerned about where you're going, you're just standing up and hitting it!

It would be wonderful if you could play that way on the golf course but it does not happen. Upon stepping up to the first tee, you begin concentrating. You think, "What do I do now? How can I do it as I did it on the practice tee?

GETTING IT TO THE GOLF COURSE

Getting your smooth practice technique to the golf course isn't easy. That's why you need to think about what you are doing while practicing. Try to create a routine of concentration while practicing, one that you can repeat on the course.

In golf, routine is important. This is why the best players have a routine they go through when lining up every shot. Watch Jack Nicklaus or Nancy Lopez. They first line up by standing behind the ball, then go into their little individual procedures of addressing the ball. They usually practice this way too, unless they're just warming up their muscles by hitting a few balls before they play.

This routine helps them transfer a smooth swing from the practice tee to the golf course. They know that if they approach the shot in the same way every time, they can do it on the golf course, just as they did on the practice tee.

THE ROUTINE

Develop your own procedure for playing a shot. I recommend that you stand behind the ball and look at where you are going. Then take your grip, set the clubface behind the ball, directly toward the target, and step into your stance. Follow this procedure on the practice tee, then repeat it on the golf course.

When putting your clubface behind the ball and toward the target, you've got to really aim it. Harvey's last words to me before a shot were always, "Take dead aim." I've never forgotten it. That's so important. If you take dead aim, you can play your best game on the golf course most of the time.

SHORT PRACTICE SESSIONS

If you don't have a lot of time to practice and can spend only a brief time at the golf course, work on your chipping and putting rather than hitting full shots.

Most courses now have practice putting greens and a great many have practice chipping greens. You'd be amazed at how your game will improve by spending just fifteen minutes a week on the practice putting and chipping greens. Such practice gives you a better feel for the correct position of the clubface. It helps your timing and builds your confidence. It's amazing, too, how your strokes around the green—your scoring strokes—will improve and how your scores will get better.

PRACTICE CHECKLIST

- Remember, only lessons and thoughtful practice will improve your game.
- Concentrate and work on something definite while practicing.
- Practice with a variety of clubs.
- Develop a routine of lining up shots and stick to it while practicing and playing.
- If practice time is limited, work on chipping and pitching.

How to Win

I've won many times, but I've lost more than I have ever won. That's why golfers have to be realistic and know that they cannot *always* win.

However, competitors in any sport, I think, want to try to win. They want to acquire the tools that will allow them to win. In golf, those tools are execution and concentration. I stress concentration because there have been many times when I may not have made the greatest swing, but I was able to maneuver the ball into a position where I knew that if I had to make a par to win the tournament, I could do it. It might not have been pretty, in the sense that the swing might not have been as great as it could have been, yet it was effective. I was able to get the ball into the hole.

This is what the tournament player needs to look for when playing a practice round. The practice round is a chance to really study the golf course. The most important research you're doing out there is figuring out where to place the ball on each hole—your tee shot, your shot to the green, or even a pitch shot—where you will best be in a position to par the hole. Standing over the ball I do not think about winning—I think about execution.

I did not begin to win until I began to learn how to PLAY. I cannot stress this too strongly. Like most young players, I worked on my swing and tried to know what I was doing with it. I tried to get better. But, if you're constantly thinking about your golf swing, you never think about what you're trying to do on the golf course. You may be thinking about trying to hit the ball with this good golf swing, but you are not thinking about the right thing, which is, "Where do I need to hit the ball?"

You begin to really compete when your thought pattern becomes,

122

"How can I best get this ball into the hole in the least amount of strokes?"

A lot of young players on the LPGA and PGA Tour make the mistake of thinking about the money. Money is their first thought because, like all of us, they need it! But this actually hinders their playing. When they start worrying about money, they freeze over putts because they're thinking, "Gosh, everytime I miss a shot I'm costing myself money!"

You can't think of winning, or losing, or making money, or not making money. You must think of what it *takes* to achieve those things.

This is what it takes to win: a fairly good, or effective, golf swing, composure, and concentration. Naturally, you won't reach a very high plateau in those departments if you don't have the *will* to win, so I'm assuming you already have that!

You must take it one step at a time and you put those steps in order. That's when you begin to learn your own golf swing, which is basically what I did. Players must also, however, guard against becoming too swing conscious. As I mentioned earlier in this book, I went through a period in the early 1960s when I was fairly successful but could not win. I'd hit the ball well on the practice tee, but I couldn't repeat that swing on the golf course. That's when Mickey Wright, one of the players I most respect, tipped me off that I was too swing conscious.

We were in Salt Lake City that week and I forgot about my swing, started thinking about how to play the golf course, and finished second in the tournament. The only time I practiced was to warm up in the morning. I did everything I could not to think about the swing, I just went out and played. I point to that one week as the time when I began to learn to play. That's when I learned to be a competitor and how to play so that when I was in a position to win, I could win.

Composure and concentration are another way of saying that you have control over your emotions, which is the other key to winning. If you get excited and think, "Oh boy!" and get really hyper about it, that's when you have to pull yourself back and think, "Yes, this is great and wonderful but I'm going to have to execute, play the holes, and do the best I can."

You don't ever think about winning. You don't think about losing. You just think about how you are going to best get this ball into the hole.

On a personal note, one of my most important wins—at least, important to me—came in 1981. I had made a change in my golf swing and consequently got into some very bad swing habits a few years before that. I had not won a tournament since 1978. It had been a long dry spell because, before that, I had won eighty-one LPGA tournaments and had not had a winless season from 1962 until 1979. The years 1979 and 1980 had been the most depressing of my golf career.

I began to see a little daylight in the last tournament of 1980. I had a couple of good rounds, so I felt that I might begin playing better during the 1981 season. The season started off really well. I had eight top-ten finishes in the first twelve tournaments. On May 3, I made quite a long putt on the last hole of the CPC Women's International at Hilton Head, South Carolina, to tie for first place, but I lost in a playoff with Sally Little.

Two weeks later, we played in the Coca-Cola Classic at the wonderful old Ridgewood Country Club in New Jersey, a course I love. I was thrilled to be getting closer and closer to winning, but it hadn't happened yet. I still had a tendency to make some funny swings and get into trouble. I shot a 69, then a 72, and I was three shots behind Alice Ritzman, the leader, going into the last round. On one of the first few holes I hit a ball into a water hazard. I remember thinking, as I walked back to the tee to replay the shot, "Stupid, dumb, dumb! Right away my chances of winning are right out the door! You can't make that kind of mistake." I bogied three holes on the front nine, then pulled it together and made four birdies on the back nine. Unfortunately for Alice, she bogied four holes coming in and I had made up seven shots. We tied, and went into a playoff.

I had felt very good, very confident, during the round. When we went into the playoff I was very nervous. I hadn't been there in awhile, so it was a good test to see whether I could hold up under pressure. At the same time, I knew what a win would mean to Alice. It would be her first victory and she had played her best golf.

We both parred the tenth, our first playoff hole. Then we teed off on the eleventh, which was a 150-yard par 3. I knew I had to hit a 7-iron because I had hit a 7-iron to that green earlier in the day and it was the correct club. I knew I had to nail it in there. Three years before I would have stood on the tee, knowing I needed to hit a certain shot and I'd think, "How the heck do I *do* it? I can't get the club back." But now I *knew* I could hit that shot because I finally had control over my swing. That was the key.

To make a long story short, I hit the ball to within nine feet of the hole and Alice hit her ball over the green. I made the birdie putt and won my first tournament in nearly three years. It was the most emotional win of my career. At times, over the previous three years, I had thought I could never win again. I really had doubts.

The win wasn't as important as *how* I won and the fact that I had been able to play. Playing well is important to me. Winning is important too, but I've won a lot, so it's not that I have to go out and prove that I can win. I had kept my self-control and executed the shot when I had to. The fact that I was still able to do that is what mattered most to me because, if you do that, you can win.

Even if you're thinking about how to best get the ball in the hole, you're still not going to do it every time. That's why you don't win every time because sometimes you're in control of your game, and sometimes you're not. Your timing may be off, or your concentration is broken, or you just can't seem to get it together that week.

When I first came on the tour in 1959, I visualized and dreamed of winning. Like most young players, I thought, "Wouldn't it be great if I could be the greatest player in the world?"

Then, reality set in and told me that you can't do this until you do something else. It's not going to just fall into your lap. You've got to earn it. You have to learn how. That's what I did, but I had a lot of help along the way.

It takes learning and, of course, the desire to learn. I think, in retrospect, that it never bothered me to lose. You're going to lose a lot more than you're going to win. You have to be willing to say, "I tried everything I could and it just wasn't good enough." This is reality. You have to accept it. Then you know that you have to do something else. You're going to have to figure out what it is that you need: Where are you not good enough? Where are you not holding together? What is your thought process? What is your execution? Did you absolutely freeze? Or did you choke?

Choking means that you cannot execute because of a lack of emotional control or because of negative thinking. You can change this, it's just a matter of going ahead and playing.

I don't remember any time when I was in the process of winning a golf tournament that I stood over a shot or a putt and thought, "I need this to win." Of course, I always knew where I stood, coming in. I knew whether I needed a par, or if I had two shots or three shots on the field. I knew where I stood especially if I was in the lead. If I was behind, and trying to catch somebody else, it didn't matter where I was; I could only play as well as I could play. I had no control over what the other player was doing. I was playing the best I could. Sometimes I won. That's really not so significant because sometimes it wasn't so much that I won, as that the other player lost, although I was glad to win.

Some people say they'd rather be behind than in the lead. Personally, I'd rather be in the lead. There's less pressure because I do have some control going down to the wire. If I don't beat myself by making a mistake, then the other player is going to have to play lights out to catch me. I've got a margin for error that the other player doesn't have.

Equipment

Golf equipment is expensive. For the best advice on clubs particularly suited to your game and physique, consult your club professional. Club professionals are trained to know what's best for their members and students. They're not just salesmen, they truly want to help their members play better golf. Fitting golfers with the right clubs is a gratifying part of the professional's job.

The pro-shop line of golf clubs is a little more expensive than golf clubs sold in department stores and sporting goods stores. That's because pro-shop lines are more carefully balanced. However, they are all good. Manufacturers generally make clubs that are very standard and of very high quality. If you're a beginning golfer, you may not want to invest heavily in golf clubs until you know you're really going to play the game. A nice beginner's set from a store will do. As you become a better player, I think it's important to go to your club professional for a more advanced set.

However, it's helpful to understand a few basic facts about golf clubs before you seek expert advice.

Golf clubs are classified as either woods or irons.

THE WOODS

The clubhead was orginally made from wood, thus the name. Today, these clubheads are made from other materials, such as lightweight steel.

I use metal woods myself because the ball jumps off the clubface somewhat faster and I get a little more distance than I do with a wood clubhead. Metal heads are also very durable and do not expand or contract with dampness in the air, which can happen to some wood heads after they have been knocked around a bit. Many tournament players continue to use wood heads because they believe they have better feel. This is entirely an individual decision. If you believe in your equipment, it gives you confidence and you play better.

Woods—the driver, 3-wood, and 4-wood—are designed for distance, although I firmly believe you don't need to sacrifice accuracy with these clubs. The more lofted woods—the 5-wood, 6-wood, and 7-wood—are for shorter shots and are very good for women and all beginning golfers because they are easier to hit than are the long irons, such as the 2-iron and 3-iron, and will carry the ball the same distance as long irons.

There's no real distance standard for wood shots. For instance, our longest hitter on the LPGA Tour, Laura Davies, can hit her driver from 300 to 330 yards. Most women professionals hit their tee shots about 230 yards. High handicappers may hit a driver less than 100 yards. Distance strictly depends on the strength and skill of the golfer.

THE IRONS

Iron clubs are also named for the material from which they are made. Some irons today are made with graphite heads but they are still called irons.

Irons are designed for the shorter shots and for accuracy. There are three types of irons: long irons, medium irons, and short irons. The long irons are generally the 1-iron, 2-iron, and 3-iron. The medium irons are the 4-iron, 5-iron, and 6-iron. The 7-iron, 8-iron, 9-iron, and wedges are the short irons. The average golfer seldom carries a 1-iron or a 2-iron. They're for longer shots and most average players find these clubs difficult to hit.

Irons have shorter shafts than woods and the shafts are joined to the clubhead at a sharper angle, which makes them more upright. Therefore the golfer must stand closer to the ball when playing an iron shot than when playing a wood. The irons also have greater loft, which means the clubface is designed at a greater angle and will hit the ball higher than will woods.

As with the woods, the distance that you hit the various irons depends completely on your own strength and the efficiency of your swing. There is no set distance to hit any club.

THE PUTTER

The putter is one of the most important clubs in the bag. You may hit your tee shots with a 3-wood, or a 5-iron, but it's likely that you'll only play your strokes on the green with a putter.

Putter designers have used a lot of imagination and putters have a wide, and sometimes weird, variety of designs. There are all shapes of clubheads and all sorts of shafts. You just have to find a putter that you like, one that feels comfortable to you.

SOME GENERAL INFORMATION ABOUT GOLF CLUBS

Golf clubs come in different lengths and weights. This is so they can be fitted to the individual golfer's size and strength.

The shafts come in a variety of flexes, which indicate how flexible or stiff the clubshafts might be. Clubshafts today are made of a variety of materials. Some clubshafts are made of the conventional steel shafts, but newer materials like graphite and fiberglass are also being used. These new materials can be very helpful to your golf game. For example, I have steel shafts on my irons but I use graphite-over-steel shafts on my woods because I find that, over a long day of tournament play, the action of a graphite shaft on my longer clubs makes them easier to swing. I'm not as tired at the end of a round as I might be if I hit many long shots, which require bigger swings with a steel shaft.

I also believe that graphite shafts, and some of the other new materials, are more forgiving. In other words, I don't have to make a perfect swing every time in order to hit a good shot. The graphite shaft has a little extra kick to it, which helps snap the clubhead through the ball at impact.

Most women are making a mistake when they use so-called women's clubs. Clubs that are called women's clubs in the catalogues are too short, for one thing.

In the past, there was a theory that women were too weak to handle men's clubs and that men's clubs were too long and too heavy for them. Most women today, however, are physically fit. The modern woman is really into exercising, strength, and staying in shape. Today, with all of the innovations in lightweight material—graphite, lightweight steel shafts, steel and graphite heads on irons and woods—there is no reason why a woman cannot use a regular length club. Most women of medium height are tall enough to handle men's-length clubs.

You can order men's clubs from a pro shop and receive clubs with a great deal of flex in the clubshafts. Those are good if you do not have a very strong physique. You can also order men's clubs of the lightest possible weight, which may also suit beginners or women without a great deal of strength. But I really believe that women, even beginners, should not use women's clubs.

EQUIPMENT BASICS FOR BEGINNERS

The basic beginner's set usually includes a driver, 3-wood, 3-iron, 5-iron, 7-iron, 9-iron, and the essential putter. That's just about all you need. Women might consider disregarding the 3-iron and ordering more woods for their bag, like a 4-wood and a 5-wood, because beginners find it difficult to hit long irons.

As I mentioned, a beginner's set from a store will do just fine. As you become a better player, talk to your club professional about equipment suited to your game and its improvement.

As you advance, you may want to buy a set with the even-numbered irons—2, 4, 6, and 8—and add additional woods. The 6-wood and 7-wood are very good for women and are great clubs to use to get out of the rough. You'll definitely want to add a sand iron, and a pitching wedge is also useful. These are called utility clubs. You will need to practice with them. They are excellent for short shots. Many beginners' sets now come with a pitching wedge.

One thing your club pro will check is the *lie* of the club best suited to your stature. The lie of the club is the angle between the shaft and the clubhead. This angle determines how far you must stand from the ball.

If you are tall, you will want a more upright lie. When the clubhead's sole, or bottom, is resting flat on the ground, its more upright lie will allow the shaft to extend properly to your hands. If you're on the short side, you will want clubs with a flatter lie, for the same reason.

TALL OR SHORT?

The taller you are, the less club you should swing because you don't need a big swing arc—you've already *got* a big arc. By less club, I mean clubs that are not particularly long or heavy.

Control and timing are the biggest problems of the tall golfer because a tall person has such a long way to go before getting to the top of the backswing. You seldom see really tall men or really tall women who are great players because they have a hard time controlling their swing. So, tall players might have better control if they did not try to swing really big clubs.

A short person should use a little longer club. They have hardly any swing arc because they are built low to the ground, so, to get more distance they would be better off using a little longer club. Patty Berg and Gene Sarazen are two classic golfers of short stature, and they used clubs longer than standard to great effect.

The weight of the club is also very important. Clubs are measured in two ways; clubhead weight and overall weight. It's important to swing a club with enough weight in the head so that you can actually feel the clubhead as you swing; however, many players choose clubs that are too heavy overall. This won't help your golf game. Heavy clubs just wear you out and decrease the effectiveness of your swing. Since each golfer has individual needs, I would suggest you consult a professional about the correct club weight for you.

Clubs are also made with a variety of grips. These basically break down into two categories: leather and rubber. Leather grips are sometimes used by very fine players because they provide great feel. But leather grips are very expensive, tend to harden, slip in wet weather, and are difficult to clean. I recommend rubber grips for most players. I use them myself, although mine are a composite rubber grip and probably too rough for most women. Regular rubber grips are very good. They won't slip easily in wet weather or when your hands are damp, they are easy to clean, and are relatively inexpensive. In fact, the cost is so reasonable that it's wise to ask your professional to put on new grips when the rubber becomes worn or hardened. Remember, the grip is your only connection to the club so it's important to keep your grips soft and tacky.

Most department stores or sporting goods stores will not allow you to try out a set of clubs before you purchase it; however, some of these stores do have driving nets where you can hit balls and experiment a bit before you make a purchase. If you are seeking an inexpensive set and have no way to try it out, you might go to a public driving range. Explain to the pro there that you're experimenting, try a few different clubs, pick out one that feels particularly good and ask the pro to weigh it and tell you the shaft flex. You can use these details when you buy your first set.

Nearly all club professionals urge their members to try new equipment before they buy.

THE LATEST AND GREATEST IN GOLF EQUIPMENT

Golf manufacturers have made a number of expensive studies about the average player and her equipment needs. They have put great effort into developing a standardized club that most people can use right off the shelf without having to buy custom-made golf clubs. This research has produced some fine new equipment.

A woman can now get a lightweight steel shaft with a good, light overall weight. Weight balance is important. That's why manufacturers go to great extremes to get good weight balance. They're trying to give you a club with enough weight to have clubhead feel, but not one that weighs a lot and feels like a sledgehammer.

A regular men's driver is 43 inches long and weighs about 13 ounces. You can have this same overall weight, or deadweight, in any club, but if all the weight is concentrated in the clubhead, the club will feel like a sledgehammer. If all the weight is in the grip, the club will have no clubhead feel at all.

When the featherlight clubs were developed a couple of years ago, the club was designed with most of the weight in the handle. The club gave the player a lot less weight to swing and players could generate great clubhead speed, but the clubs had no feel so you didn't know where the clubhead was going. You had no control because it was like swinging a toothpick.

I trust the clubmakers. Manufacturers have now developed heel-toe weighting. This is a special weight distribution and a tremendous innovation for the average player because if the ball starts to go left after being struck with this type of club, it will straighten out. If it starts to go right, it will straighten out. This is a very forgiving club. It is much easier to hit.

The best innovation for women in recent years is the improved development in deadweight, or overall weight. That has impressed me the most over the years, especially since I've gotten older and I'm not quite as strong as I was.

The deadweight has become so much lighter, but clubs still retain good clubhead feel. My clubs still have the same feel as the heavier clubs I was swinging when I was younger.

FINDING THE RIGHT CLUBS

I stay with the tried and true in my own golf equipment. I use metal heads on my woods but metal heads are not anything new. Driving range operators used them on rental clubs years and years ago. But the metal has been improved and is now a lightweight steel, or a composite steel. It's an easier club to hit.

My driver is 43½ inches long, ½ inch longer than the standard men's length, but my deadweight is a full ounce lighter than standard. My deadweight is 12 ounces, standard is 13 ounces. That doesn't sound like much but, over a period of seventy-two holes, that's a lot! It takes a lot less effort to swing the club in order to get the same results. I've always felt that it's not how far I can hit the ball when I hit it well, but how far I can hit the ball when I miss it.

I tried several drivers before finding one that I really like. I would hope that anyone changing clubs would have an opportunity to try them out first, because golf clubs are very expensive. It's also hard for anyone to recommend clubs unless the player has a chance to try them out. Feel has so much to do with the decision, and how you actually *hit* the ball has a lot to do with it.

You may think you need a stiffer shaft, or a shaft with more kick in it. Maybe you do, but until you try that kind of shaft it's impossible to know if it's right for you. Just as I said about my own game and my own clubs, it's not how far you hit the ball when you hit it well—because you can hit almost any club a long way when you connect solidly and time it right—but, when trying a new club, if you miss it shorter than you did with your old club, you probably should not change.

When I took up the game, my teacher, Harvey Penick, told me, "I blame you first, me second, and the equipment third." The club manufacturers have made clubs that you should be able to hit if you have the right swing. If you have a problem, it's not necessarily the club. You are just shifting the burden of guilt.

Remember, you can spend a fortune on golf clubs and not improve your game.

BEGINNER'S CHECKLIST

- Buy clubs at a store or pro shop where you will be allowed to try them out before your purchase.
- Buy your clubs from someone who knows about the most important equipment factors: swing weight, flex, and proper lie.
- Avoid buying clubs that are too heavy, but choose lightweight men's clubs over women's. Ask yourself if you could swing these clubs throughout a four-hour round of golf and not get tired.

   Swing weights are measured by letters and numbers. Stronger women can use a D-0 or D-1 swing weight. Average women will be happier with a C-8 swing weight, or a C-9, which is slightly heavier but not as heavy as the D-0 or D-1. Senior women (in golf, that's women aged fifty and up) might consider the C-8 or C-9.
- If you are strong, buy clubs with an R or Regular men's shaft flex. Never, ever, buy an S or Stiff shaft! If you have average strength or if you're a senior player, buy clubs with an A shaft, which is somewhat more flexible than the Regular shaft. Ask your pro.

BEGINNER'S CHECKLIST (continued)

- Buy clubs of the proper lie. You can check this yourself: Grip the club, flex your knees very slightly, and let your arms hang naturally in front of your torso. When the clubhead sits flat on the ground, does the shaft extend comfortably to your hands? The clubhead must be truly flat on the ground, without the heel or toe of the clubhead in the air. Then, if the club extends above your hands, the lie is too upright. If you must bend over, the lie is too flat.
- Buy clubs with rubber grips.

PART II

My Life in Golf

Beginnings

The Ladies Professional Golf Association is my life. It has been my life for thirty years.

As I've traveled around the world playing golf, some of the people I've met have asked if I have regrets. They have been concerned that my involvement in my career has caused me to give up the idea of having a family. It wasn't a great sacrifice. I didn't give up a family, I decided I didn't want one. I freely made the decision to dedicate myself to professional golf. No one held a gun to my head; the hours that I spent on the practice tee were hours I *wanted* to spend on the practice tee. I wanted to be a good player, I wanted to get better, and I didn't mind putting in the hours to get there.

When I look back on my life in golf, what satisfies me most is that the length of my career has given me the opportunity to play with so many of history's greatest players. I was there when the greats of yesteryear were playing, so I got to know Patty Berg, Sam Snead, Byron Nelson, Louise Suggs, Betsy Rawls, Mickey Wright, Betty Jameson, Mary Lena Faulk, and Jackie Pung. In my own era, I've played with the greats like Jack Nicklaus, Carol Mann, Sandra Haynie, Donna Caponi, Marlene Hagge, and Judy Rankin.

Because I am still playing today, I know an era of golfers who will still be playing when I quit. I'm sure Nancy Lopez will be there as well as Beth Daniel, Betsy King, and Pat Bradley. I also know the younger players who are just coming into their own, the champions of the future. Years after I retire, some of the people I've met will still be playing and I'll be able to watch their careers.

Because my career has spanned so many eras of great golfers, I was there in the early days of the LPGA Tour. I knew our greatest players and played with them all, except Babe. Babe Zaharias died before I went on tour and, if I have one regret, it's that I never met her. When I was a youngster, I followed Babe's career in the newspapers even before I began to play the game.

THE OPENING ROUNDS AT HOME

I was fifteen when I played my first round of golf. I was so terrible that I played by myself for an entire year before I became brave enough to play with anyone else!

We lived in Jal, New Mexico, a little community that had sprung up in the cattle country near the western border of Texas.

Since my folks weren't members of the country club, I paid green fees. Like many golf courses in that part of the West, Jal Country Club was first built with sand greens. By the time I started to play, in about 1955, we had cottonseed greens and a short time later the greens were converted to bent grass.

Junior players were only allowed to play on weekends. During the week, I'd gather up a few golf balls and hit practice shots in a cow pasture.

I practiced and played for about a year before Mother and Dad decided golf wasn't a passing fancy. They joined the country club for me so I could play all the time and I began to play with my aunt and uncle, Nell and George Addison. George was a wonderful athlete, a scratch golfer with a beautiful touch around the greens, and he won almost everything in our area. Nell was a good player too and won the club championship and a lot of local tournaments.

My father, Morris Whitworth, played basketball in school but I don't think he was a serious player and I never really thought of Dad as an athlete.

My mother, Dama Robinson Whitworth, was athletic. She was terribly competitive and still is for that matter! She played high school basketball. Mother's team used to travel from one little town to another, playing against local teams, and I'm sure she was a pretty good player.

I was born September 27, 1939, in Monahans, Texas, where Dad was working for a lumber company. I was the youngest of three daughters. Carlynne was the eldest, then Evelynne, then me. Shortly after I was born we moved back to Jal and I lived there until I went on the LPGA Tour in 1959.

My mother's family homesteaded that part of the country. Her father opened a grocery store in Jal and they did some farming. They had cows and pigs, and I remember playing in the barn when I was growing up. My sisters and I used to try to ride calves and

My mother, Dama Whitworth, has been a staunch supporter through good
times and bad. This was one of the good times, when I was inducted into
the Texas Golf Hall of Fame.

horses. We watched my grandfather butcher a hog and we'd swim
in the big tanks where they watered the livestock in the pasture.

Local lore says that Jal was named for the J-A-L ranch brand. It
eventually became an oil and gas town and the story was that all
pipelines led to Jal. Because of our refineries, almost all of the
natural gas in the Southwest came through Jal, so we had a pros-
perous little town, in that respect. Jal never got very big and at its
peak had about 5,000 residents.

My father's father, "Whit," opened a lumber company in town and Dad worked for him for a while and, later, for several gas companies. My grandmother, Jessie Whitworth, bought a hardware store. Mother worked in the store and Dad kept Jessie's books at night, as he did for several businesses around town.

My folks were productive working people, and very active in the community. Mother had a big family, eight brothers and sisters. At one time, my cousins and aunts and uncles made up about half the population of Jal. You could hardly talk to us about anybody in town—they were probably our relatives.

Mother and Dad eventually bought Whitworth Hardware, which they ran for years. Dad was very involved in local politics. He was on the city council for years and was elected Mayor three times.

Dad has written a humor column for *The Jal Record*, our weekly newspaper, for many years. Mother is very active in the church, in community and charity organizations, and in Democratic politics.

FINDING THE GAME

I played all sports as I was growing up, but mostly in sandlot games. I hated physical education because we never really got to do anything but run around the basketball court, which didn't appeal to me at all, so I joined the band. I played the bass drum. My sister Carlynne was a drummer and she was sort of my idol; anything she did, I had to do. I don't know that I could have played another instrument, but I was always the biggest girl in school so I could carry the drum.

I was on the Jal High School tennis team and I was fairly proficient at tennis, depending upon the competition. In fact, that's how I started playing golf. Some of my tennis friends one day insisted that we play golf. I used my grandfather's golf clubs. Whit had been a pretty good golfer who shot in the 80s.

I'll never forget that first round. I was *terrible*, but that made golf a real challenge. Because other sports had come to me so naturally, I was fascinated with this game that I couldn't master. Golf also appealed to me because I didn't have to rely on another person in order to play. It was just me against the golf course and I played against myself. How well I played didn't depend on anyone else because I had par to shoot at.

In those days, the Jal Women's Golf Association traveled to quite a few little tournaments, and the members were nice enough to take me with them. My family wasn't poor, but with two other children there wasn't a lot of extra money lying around for golf. I paid my own expenses and the members of the women's golf association saw to it that I went to tournaments by letting me ride with them. I'm sure I wasn't as grateful then as I am now. As the years go by, I look back and think about how great it was that I had nice people like that in my life.

After playing for about a year, I took lessons from Dode Forrester at Hobbs Country Club, about forty miles from home. He taught me things that I use today, including a strong hip move on the downswing.

My first real mentor was Hardy Loudermilk, our pro at Jal Country Club. Hardy taught me a lot, then did something that showed unusual generosity and humility and caused me to take what was probably the most important step of my career. When I was seventeen, Hardy said, "I don't know enough to take you where you need to be."

With the late Hardy Loudermilk, my first teacher and a good friend, the night I was inducted into the Texas Sports Hall of Fame, 1982.

Hardy had met Harvey Penick, the golf professional in Austin, Texas, who was one of the world's best and most respected teachers. Hardy said that I had advanced to a point where I needed more instruction if I was going to be a really good player, so he called Harvey and set up an appointment for me.

Mother and I drove the 450 miles to Austin and, on this first trip, I spent four days taking lessons from Harvey. I hit practice balls from sunup to sundown. Harvey would keep an eye on me, even while he was giving someone else a lesson, and Mother sat behind me on the practice tee taking notes. At night, we would go to a driving range and I would practice until the lights were turned off. Harvey would also telephone Hardy back in Jal, tell him what I was working on and, when I returned home, Hardy would watch me to make sure I followed Harvey's instructions. Most of what I know about the golf swing, I learned from Harvey Penick.

In 1957, I won the New Mexico State Women's Championship in Farmington, New Mexico. The tournament committee had planned to present a beautiful turquoise necklace to the winner. Typically like a seventeen-year-old, I wanted a trophy. The committee kept the necklace and sent a trophy to me, which I thought was just outstanding. Of course, today I wish I had taken the necklace!

On the Road With the LPGA

In 1958, I won the state championship again and I began to meet some of the women golf professionals.

Wilson Sporting Goods often sent Betsy Rawls and Mickey Wright to small towns to play exhibitions. This was thirty years ago, and a young player who showed promise was big stuff back then, especially in our part of the West, so I was invited to play in these exhibitions. In our part of the country, from Amarillo to Pecos, it was nothing to jump in the car and drive 400 miles to play golf, especially if you could play with the real stars of the game.

In Hobbs, New Mexico, I played with Betsy. I played with Mickey in Hobbs and then in Pecos. It became like a regular tour! Every time Mickey came to that area, there I'd be.

After we played an exhibition in Amarillo, I asked Mickey if I could talk to her. We went into the pro's office and I told her I was very seriously thinking of turning pro. Mickey thought, however, that, at nineteen, I was still too young for the tour. She advised me to wait a year and to continue to work with Harvey on my swing. I believed her. If Mickey said it, this was the way to go.

However, I had financial backers if I turned pro, which was unusual for that day. Dad, Hardy, George Blocker, who owned a gas company, and George Kendrick, who worked for El Paso Natural Gas, had agreed to put up $5,000 a year for three years. The only stipulation was that I was to give them 50 percent of my winnings during that time, which turned out to be nothing. When we discussed my career at home, Mother and Dad said, ''Well, let's just do it.'' I agreed. And that was it.

I sent my application to the LPGA in January, 1959. Mother and I hit the highways in my little green Plymouth. My first professional tournament was the Mayfair Open in Sanford, Florida. We believed all the propaganda about how warm Florida was in the winter and almost froze to death. It was so cold that Mother and I would hurry back to the motel after I played, jump into our beds, and pull the covers over our heads to get warm.

Two other players turned pro that year: Mary Ann Reynolds and Barbara Romack. Their amateur records were much better than mine. Barbara, a former U.S. Women's Amateur Champion, was a great player, and Mary Ann had won some big tournaments. You band together when you're the new kids on tour, so Mary Ann and I became friends and that helped me because I was quite shy. Eventually I got to know some of the other girls and some of the nice people in our tournament towns.

Those were great times. Our purses were meager by today's standards, but you could make a living, and the top players made a very good living. Of necessity, because we were always on the road and there were only a few dozen players, we were closer too. After a tournament, we'd always sit around together and have a party. Usually the winner would buy the drinks because she was the only one who had any money!

We ran all the tournaments ourselves; we had a pairings committee, a rules committee, and a course set-up committee. We even did our own publicity. In fact, all of us were very public-relations conscious. We really believed in the association and its potential, but we felt that the only way we could really sell it was to capture the good will of our galleries and sponsors. We worked hard to be friendly, cooperated with the press, and attended all of the Pro-Am cocktail parties. It worked. We got a lot of grass roots support from golf fans and we were able to keep our tour going. I believe very firmly that this approach still works, and I try to foster that sort of spirit today.

We went to great lengths to keep up our public image. We knew we had to look sharp, neat and well ironed, with shoes polished. We even had fines for temperamental outbursts. If you threw a club you'd get tabbed for $50. One of our players, JoAnne Prentice, better known as Fry, had a terrible temper. The rule was, if you tossed a club, it couldn't touch the ground or you'd be fined. One day Fry missed an iron shot and heaved a club into the air. Just about the time the club reached the peak of its arc, Fry remembered the $50 fine, frantically circled under the falling club, and made a diving catch worthy of Willie Mays.

In off-hours, we often split into two groups, the bridge players and the poker players. I wasn't real good at either, but it was a nice way to pass the time between tournament rounds. Betty Jameson, the Hall-of-Famer and former U.S. Open Champion, was a fanatical

What a surprise! I made this forty-foot putt to win the LPGA championship. (*William Morrissey*)

hearts player. She even wore a green eyeshade when she played.

She may have worn the eyeshade because she had great peripheral vision. For that reason, it was difficult to play golf with Betty. She could see so many things going on around her that she was easily distracted by other players. I have great peripheral vision too. I can see a lot of movement to the side even when I'm looking straight ahead, and it can be very distracting. So, Betty had a reputation of moving her playing partners around. She'd be standing over a putt, head anchored, eyes looking straight at the ball, and without moving, she'd gesture frantically for some player thirty yards away to move! For that reason, tournament golf, with its galleries and other distractions, was difficult for her.

Years later, Betty remarked, "Too bad I never played with you."

"Yes, you did," I said. "I just stayed in the trees on every hole so I wouldn't bother you!"

With old friends Carol Mann and Sandra Haynie when I won the World Series of Golf in 1968.

Betty had a very solid swing, very compact. She was built very solidly and just looked like she was going to hit the ball well when she stood up to it. Good grip, good address position. The only thing that hurt her was her timing, which would sometimes get a little fast. But I enjoyed watching her play.

Mary Lena Faulk was another of our good players. Mary Lena hit a little draw and that ball just ran like a little bunny. She was a great fairway wood player and had a really impressive short game, better than that of most players. She's a wonderful lady and never had a bad word to say about anybody. Under the most trying circumstances, she'd find something good in everything. You could depend on Mary Lena.

I loved watching these great women golfers play and learned a

Making my acceptance speech after winning at home, the Dallas Civitan Open in 1968. (*Associated Press*)

lot by studying them carefully, particularly Patty Berg, Mickey Wright, Betsy Rawls, and Louise Suggs.

I'd watch Suggs and wonder, "How is she so consistent? Why is she always able to hit her shots the same way? Why does she have the same routine while putting, chipping, and hitting full shots?"

Louise's routine never varied. All good players have that routine because it helps build your confidence. Timing and feel change from day to day and, if you go through the same routine, you have a better chance of hitting the ball the same way each time.

I have a great deal of respect for Louise. Her execution was so great, she was like a machine. She wasn't a flashy player or one who comes crashing out of the trees all the time. She executed her shots so well that she was seldom in trouble. Louise and I have sort of the same temperament; we don't talk a lot on the golf course, so she was very pleasant to play with.

Betsy Rawls was another player I've always admired. Her record speaks for itself. She's a four-time U.S. Women's Open Champion, a member of the LPGA Hall of Fame, and today remains a key administrator in women's golf.

As a player, Betsy had a good swing but she had one of the best short games I've ever seen. She had a very soft touch around the green and a wonderful approach to putting. Long ago, I read of her putting philsophy in a magazine article and I've followed it since. Betsy always tried to putt the ball to the hole, rather than stroking a putt past the hole, because she felt that such a stroke helped her take advantage of all the corners.

Betsy has a terrific mind. She was Phi Beta Kappa at the University of Texas, and a great thinker on the golf course. Although I never talked to her about her course strategy, I assume that she played the percentages. She never gave up. You never knew if she was shooting 60 or 90 because she was trying so hard on every shot. I believe her great reasoning ability helped her develop that attitude.

I have many wonderful friends in Japan. Here I'm receiving a set of pearls at the 1986 Mazda Japan Classic.

Another thing that made Betsy a great player was her ability to be unemotional on the golf course. I hardly ever saw her show any temper or any elation, which is good because it's hard to play well when you're going through a lot of highs and lows.

Her short game was exceptional. She could get the ball up and down from almost anywhere. I'll never forget seeing her get it up and down from the side of a mountain. We were playing Esmerelda Golf Course in Spokane, Washington. On a short par 4, dogleg right around a mountain, Betsy cut the corner a bit too close on her drive and the ball bounded up the side of the hill. We weren't even sure we could find the ball. When we did find it, Betsy analyzed the situation and proceeded to create some type of shot, managed to hit the ball close to the green, then chipped it close to the hole and made her putt for a par. There was no quit. As long as she saw some way, she'd do it. You could just see her mind clicking away.

That was early in my career and it made a big impression on me.

When Betsy retired, she became the LPGA's first Tournament Director. She was extremely good at it—good with people and good at making policies and judgments. She would never allow her personal feelings to interfere with her decisions as to what was fair and right.

I have a great deal of respect and admiration for Betsy and today consider her a good friend. I feel very close to her, in the sense that I shared her career with her and watched her put her imprint on LPGA policies that we still use today.

What I most admire about these women—Betsy, Louise, and others—is that, had it not been for their desire to play, we would not have a tour today. They started from zero. Of course, they had a lot of help, from the sporting goods companies, for example. That brings me to Patty Berg. Patty worked for Wilson Sporting Goods before a women's pro tour existed. Patty got Wilson's support for the tour through her personal dedication, the respect that the Wilson people had for her playing ability, and their personal fondness for her. For these women to start from scratch in 1950 and establish a tour that is still going today, and doing quite well, is a marvelous thing. I can't think of many of us who would have that much gumption and fortitude today.

So, at nineteen, I was a rookie on the LPGA Tour, and thrilled to be there. I was a pro! I hadn't signed with an equipment company, but Wilson was giving golf equipment to me. I had a big new golf bag and a shag bag of practice balls. My game, however, didn't match my enthusiasm and, as the season progressed, I became very discouraged. I almost quit during my first year. I was playing terribly and not making any money, so I drove home to discuss the future with Mother and Dad. They convinced me to give it a little more time, to keep trying. I returned to the tour feeling a little better about my career. The next week, in Asheville, North Carolina, I tied with two other players for the last prize check. We split $100. I had won $33. I called home, feeling as good as if I'd won the tournament.

Knowing Patty Berg

Of all the people I've known in golf, the person I most admire and the one who has influenced me most is Patty Berg.

The tour in 1959 was very different from the big show that we have today. There were so few of us then, probably thirty strong, that we saw a lot of each other. Those times gave me a wonderful opportunity to just be around these great players, and that's how I began to know Patty.

Patty Berg has had a long and wonderful working relationship with Wilson, the firm which helped start the LPGA Tour. She is the dean of Wilson's golf staff and we used to say, affectionately, that there are two things Patty loves, God and the Wilson Sporting Goods Company!

Patty and I are great, great friends today, but when I was a young player, she scared me to death.

In my rookie year, Wilson wanted to sign a staff of women pros to represent their Walter Hagen division. Wilson was looking at Mary Ann Reynolds and a few others. I had not yet proven myself as a player. I'd had a few good tournaments but had no amateur record to speak of and certainly hadn't set the world on fire. Fortunately, when Wilson sought to hire a Hagen staff, someone must have said, "What about Whitworth?"

In those days, the MacGregor, Wilson, and Spalding equipment companies were known as the big three. At that time, when looking at potential staff players, the companies did background checks. Without my knowledge, Wilson began looking into my background, my family, and my teaching professional. I passed, evidently, and Wilson planned to offer a contract to me when we played in Illinois, although I knew nothing about it.

Spalding, meanwhile, was taking a look at Murle Breer. The

My friend Patty Berg inducting me into the Texas Golf Hall of Fame.

week of the tournament I was helping Murle carry her clubs into the clubhouse and I had a box of Spalding irons under my arm. Patty saw me with the Spalding box and nearly had cardiac arrest.

"Drop those clubs!" Patty yelled.

My mouth flew open.

"Those are Spaldings! Drop those clubs!" she shouted. "You're not going to play those, are you?"

"No, I'm just carrying them for Murle," I said.

"Well, get *rid* of them!" Patty yelled.

I dropped the clubs.

Patty was very distraught. She later told me that the president and vice-president of Wilson were coming to the club to sign me to a contract. She had gone out on a limb to support me, and here I was carrying Spalding irons into the clubhouse. I managed not to foul up again and, that week, signed a contract with Wilson, joining the Walter Hagen staff.

Under a Wilson contract, an LPGA player had to do clinics and exhibitions. That was one way in which the companies subsidized the tour. The only way Wilson could keep the players on tour was to schedule exhibitions for them and pay the players for these appearances. Sometimes they'd pull players off the tour for exhibitions, which wasn't good because we had so few players, but that was part of the contract. It wasn't an option. When the companies booked you, you had to go.

I've done hundreds, maybe thousands, of clinics and exhibitions. One year, Carol Mann and I had to pick up part of the schedule of two other players who got sick. Carol and I did seventy or eighty appearances between October and January. That experience nearly drove us wild, but the clinics were great, great training.

Patty Berg, of course, was the greatest clinician of all time. Each staff member had to go through a six-week training program with Patty in Fort Myers, Florida, her winter home. That was the grandest thing that ever happened to me. I just know in my heart that, without her teaching, I would not have been as successful as I have been.

Patty taught us to play different types of shots for our clinics: hooks, fades, punch shots, high shots, low shots, and bunker shots. I was a terrible bunker player but, with her help, I became much, much better. That training, and doing those clinics, was a wonderful way to learn more about the game.

We never went home in those days. If we had an off-week during the season, Wilson would send us on the road to do a series of one-day stands where we would give our clinic and play a nine-hole exhibition. We learned to be poised in front of galleries and we practiced the shots all the time because we knew we'd have to hit them in a clinic. Today, I don't believe I would practice hitting high and low shots, draws and fades. People would ask us questions during the clinics, which also helped our games because it made us stop and think about what we were doing.

We used to have a big LPGA clinic at each tournament. Patty would be master of ceremonies and we players would hit the shots. It was very embarrassing, not because of the gallery, but because the other players were sitting in the front row awaiting their turn to hit. While they waited, they'd make these terrible teasing comments about the swing of the player on the tee, so you were just mortified when you knew it was your turn.

Patty made it worse. She'd give the rookies a hard time, all in good fun. She often made me hit the long irons, which are very hard to hit, especially when you've been sitting in a chair for 30 minutes and suddenly have to stand up and hit this long iron in front of people.

She had also heard that I hit a 2-wood, a club so hard to hit that very few men pros use them. The 2-wood was a rare club because it's a fairway wood with very little loft, which makes it extremely hard to get the shot airborne. What Patty didn't know was that I used the 2-wood as an occasional replacement for my driver. I hit a 2-wood only from a tee, never from a fairway lie.

In one clinic, in front of the other players, Patty told me to hit the 2-wood off of the ground.

"Patty, I can't hit it off the ground!" I moaned.

She made me do it anyway. Right there, in front of a gallery and all my peers, I scuffed the shot.

Patty just said, "Well, sit down."

She never asked me to hit the 2-wood again.

Patty was always testing her jokes on us. We'd listen to the LPGA clinic and—this is a great tribute to her—we heard the same jokes every week but Patty's delivery was so great that we couldn't help but get tickled. We knew it was coming, but we always had to laugh. Patty loved it, and if we started laughing, she'd start laughing. Now and then she'd spring a new joke on us and we'd really break up.

Patty always teased the Wilson players. Wilson was owned by the Wilson Meat Packing Company and she told us that if we didn't start playing better, we'd have to go to work in the meat packing plant.

Patty Berg had great determination and was a very tough competitor. She grew up playing football with the neighborhood boys, including Bud Wilkinson, who would one day be the coach at Oklahoma State. Her father was very supportive of her athletic ability, but it was hard back in those days and she had to fight the barriers that existed for women athletes.

As a youngster, Patty was a speed skater and played baseball and football. Those skills carried over into her game. She had a wonderful golf swing, although not as spectacular as, say, Mickey Wright's. Her swing wasn't as powerful as Mickey's but it was repetitive. Just as when watching Mickey, Louise Suggs, and Betsy Rawls, you could close your eyes and know that Patty was going to swing the same way every time. Those four were like machines.

Patty was a great all-around golfer. She didn't play just one shot well. She was a great sand-wedge and pitching-wedge player and had a great touch around the green. I saw her play some shots that were just outstanding.

I learned an awful lot from Patty's demeanor. She handles herself so well, has great values, and high standards. She's very religious, a very generous person with the public, and she treats everyone alike—sponsors, gallery, players, and caddies. Patty never spoke badly of anyone and always showed me the other side of things when I was upset about something in the association or about my lousy play that week. If it was my swing, and she saw a flaw, she'd point it out. If it was an LPGA issue, she'd use her intelligence and experience to help me by pointing out options.

Whenever I was in a slump, Patty was always right there. It's wonderful to have a friend like that when you're questioning your ability. A slump teaches me time and again that fame is fleeting, and sometimes *friends* are fleeting. I went through a lot of slumps, some were very discouraging. You work your way out of them, hopefully, but even if I didn't, I knew that Patty would think no less of me. You get past that point in a friendship.

Most assuredly, because of Patty the LPGA is what it is today. She had help, but she established a very high level of play, a high level of standards, and an example of how to conduct yourself as a person and as a sportsperson. Patty created a lot of fans for women's golf. To this day, everywhere I go I meet someone who knows or has seen Patty Berg.

I would give her at least 50 percent of the credit for the development of the LPGA. Babe Zaharias was wonderful in her own way and her flamboyance generated a lot of attention. Babe was a great athlete before she turned to golf and brought her following with her to women's golf but, as I understand it, Babe didn't do that much work in the association. She wanted to rule, but she didn't want to be president or to do the mundane chores.

Babe's way was to call up a friend and say, ''Harry, why don't you put up $5,000 and we'll have a tournament.'' Those tournaments didn't last very long because they had no solid basis. I really credit Patty and some of the others for doing the legwork and selling the LPGA in a businesslike manner. Patty's a good business person. She could see where she needed to lead us and she took us down those roads. Those contributions are difficult to explain because they seem dull and unimportant. Golf needed players like Babe, but more than anything we needed a solid base on which to grow. That's what Patty gave us.

In 1988, I was given the LPGA's annual ''Patty Berg Award'' at the McDonald's Championship in Wilmington, Delaware. That night meant more to me than almost any other because of what Patty represents and how much she means to me. She really made me mad, though, because she got emotional at the presentation! That made me emotional, and I hadn't planned on that!

The LPGA named the award for Patty to honor her for what she has done for us. The ''Patty Berg Award'' probably means more to me than it might mean to other players because of my personal feelings for Patty and because of what she has done for the LPGA.

The LPGA means so much to me and, to me, Patty Berg *is* the LPGA.

The LPGA Tour, Then and Now

I have strong feelings for the charter members and players who came before me because the LPGA means so much to me. By choice, the tour has been my life and the LPGA has furnished me with a wonderful life. If I died tomorrow, just think, what a life I've had!

Throughout most of my career, I've been involved in the political side of our association. Like the other early players, I had to be involved because we ran the LPGA for many years. We did just about everything. In my first year on the tour, we were between commissioners. Marilynn Smith, one of our veteran players, was LPGA president that year, and Marilynn acted as president, commissioner, and social director. Marilynn got sponsors for our tournaments and signed the contracts. All the players were involved in trying to get new tournaments and, if we knew anyone or had good contacts, we used them.

We had no paid staff, but we did have one good volunteer, Eileen Stulb. Eileen lived in Augusta, Georgia, where we played the Titleholders', one of our most important championships. She was in the advertising business and became good friends with some of our members because she worked on the tournament and was also a good amateur player. We hired her—although I don't believe we paid her—and Eileen became sort of our headquarters. We had our correspondence sent to her and she put together a good brochure for the press, which had pictures and bios of the players. That's how we had to run the association for a long time.

As a young player, I was assigned to my first LPGA job, the pairings committee. I was delighted that the other players thought enough of me to let me do the work, although they probably thought, "Here's a new sucker, we'll get her to do the pairings."

156

There were so few players that pairing them wasn't a problem. As soon as we finished playing, our committee would get the scores from the scoreboard in the order that the players finished, then make the pairings. When Mother was with me on the tour, she worked as my "assistant." While I played, she would record the scores as they came in, then we'd go to the locker room and together we would set up pairings for the next day's round. Mother loved it and, because she was right there when everyone finished, she usually knew more about the tournament standings than I did! Mothers were a big part of the tour in the early days. JoAnne Prentice, Beth Stone, Marlene Hagge, and Alice Bauer, who were sisters, all had their mothers on the tour at different times. One year we had a little exhibition tournament at Belvedere Par 3 in West Palm Beach, and my mother and Jackie Pung's mother spent most of the tournament in the grill, slapping together sandwiches to sell to the galleries.

I next served on the tournament committee. We'd go out with the club's green superintendent and help set up the course, marking areas for ground-under-repair, and that sort of thing. The green superintendent, however, set the tees and flagsticks. Until the late 1960s, we were forced to play from the back of the men's tees because the superintendants didn't want our players to shoot better scores than their good male members. That was standard procedure. By the final round, we were often hanging off the backs of the tees. We never played from the ladies' tees until Lenny Wirtz became our executive director in the late 1960s and shortened the courses.

Gloria Armstrong was our treasurer. When Gloria finished playing her final round in a tournament, she would work out the money breakdown. If a player needed money, Gloria would make out the check on the spot.

Lenny Wirtz did some good things for the LPGA, such as setting up our first real office, which was in Cincinnati, and hiring our first LPGA secretary.

Today we have a paid staff of about twenty-five people. It's a whole new ball game. In the old days, we could put a tournament together in a matter of weeks, whereas now it takes one year. In those days we never knew how many events we'd play because we'd begin the year with an incomplete schedule. We'd start with a few off-weeks on the schedule, then those weeks would suddenly be filled.

When we left home for the start of the new season, we stayed on the tour for nine months. We were on the road all the time, never flying home or taking a week off. Of course, there was no reason to take a week off from tournaments because, with our meager schedule, we had a lot of weeks off! To miss a tournament in those days was just taboo. With only thirty to thirty-five players, we needed everybody, and I mean every*body*! We needed bodies!

And so, through the early years I served on the committees and held most of the offices, including two terms as LPGA president. Today, we may not have the same problems that we had in the early years, but problems always exist and we have to deal with them. In 1989, I was elected president of the Ladies Professional Golf Association for the third time.

In 1987, some of the players got together and told me they wanted me to run for vice-president in 1988, with the idea of being president the following year. I never sought the office, because I have great confidence in our players—their motivations are honorable—but if the membership wanted me to run, then that was fine. That's basically why I ran; the players felt that I had something more to contribute. So much has been given to me that serving as president is no great sacrifice. Nothing I do can compare to what I've taken out of the game. I was reluctant only in that I do think it's time that the younger players take more of an interest.

Involving some of our better young players in the association is one of my goals. These players will have to lead. It has always been and will always be that way because the public respects them. Involvement of our good players is important because younger players always look to them and say, "Lead me."

When you become a top player, the responsibility of leadership lands in your lap, whether you like it or not. We've had a sort of backsliding in that area in the LPGA, and I'd like to see more of our good young players assume the responsibility before I retire.

Today's players have a different attitude than the players of years past. This is not a criticism, it's just a fact. In earlier days, we played every week because we wanted to play. The money wasn't that great. We had to play in order to just make a living. Even if we won, we weren't going to make a fortune. The pace wasn't as fast, the pressure wasn't as intense, but you played for the love of it.

If you thought you were going to make a lot of money playing golf in those days, you were crazy! There just wasn't much money to be made. If you won, however, you could make a good living in comparison to what other jobs of that era offered to women. So professional golf was a viable alternative to a nine-to-five job. I've talked to some amateurs who didn't turn pro back in the old days. They say, "There just wasn't any money in it." When you see today's players quoted, it is evident that money is very much on their minds. Today, money is a big motivation, which is why we have so many more players.

Wright, Nicklaus, Hagge, Snead, Lopez, and Friends

MICKEY WRIGHT

Of all the players I've watched, men and women, nobody could swing a golf club as well as Mickey Wright. In her overall game, she was just head and shoulders above everyone.

Mickey was a great student of the game, and still is. She developed a swing in which she achieved tremendous clubhead speed and positioning. It was a repititious swing and, to me, looked the same every time. Mickey could do almost everything: She could play trouble shots well, she could play any shot she wanted, and she had terrific emotional control. She had to learn all of this, just as Ben Hogan and Sam Snead developed their swings, but for pure, explosive power, Mickey was the most impressive.

Mickey brought a higher standard to the golf swing that no one has been able to duplicate, man or woman. Hers was a swing that combined the mechanical with "swing," that is, rhythm. Her mechanics were just great and yet she would also swing the club. Hogan was more mechanical, and that was the difference in his swing and Mickey's swing, although Hogan's was good too. Snead was more of a swinger than a mechanical player.

As a sports figure, I would put Mickey in almost the same category as Bobby Jones. She is very gracious, handles herself so well, and is so nice to people. She had a lot of charm. Besides the great swing and the great golf that she played, I hope that people will also remember her as a very kind, gracious lady. I think that's very important. There's a lot of class there.

As a young player, I was just thrilled out of my mind when I

What a thrill it was to play with my friend Mickey Wright (center) in 1985 when we became the first women to play in ''The Legends,'' the men's senior tournament in Austin, Texas.

was paired with Mickey. It was such a pleasure to be inside the ropes with her because I knew I was in for a treat. She was always very gracious and kind to her playing partners, just a very pleasant individual to play with. Although we played together many, many times, I never played with her with the idea of beating her. Everyone has a bad day now and then, and when she had one, I might happen to have the lower score if I was playing well.

In 1985, Mickey and I were the first women to play in ''The Legends of Golf'' tournament, the men's senior event in Austin, Texas. It was the first time that we really shared our golf. By that I mean that we weren't competing against each other. We were a team and discussed strategy and the characteristics of the golf course. We got along so well and I had a wonderful time. I thought it was great that Mickey came out of retirement for the world to see how great she really is.

In recent years, through a mutual friend, we have struck up our old friendship. We talk on the phone periodically and she has come to Dallas and spent time in my home. We visit back and forth. Even though we played together on the tour, I came in at the end of Mickey's era and, in experience, I never really felt like a contemporary of Mickey, Betsy Rawls, or Patty Berg. Today Mickey and I are much closer.

JACK NICKLAUS

I was pretty impressed the first time I played with Jack Nicklaus. He shot 59! We were playing in a charity exhibition in 1973 at the Breakers Golf Club, a Donald Ross layout in Palm Beach. The course was short, but it had small, elevated greens, so it was great fun to play.

I had heard that Jack couldn't play a wedge shot and that his short game wasn't all that great, but that theory didn't hold true that day. He hit some wonderful wedge shots and his short game was just outstanding. That's what impressed me.

Jack brought golf to another plateau, took it to another level, as Arnold Palmer did before him. Arnold was more charismatic and flamboyant, while Jack was a more serious player. What I most admire about Jack is how he handled himself when he first went on tour. He was a pretty hefty young guy and he was also beating Palmer, who was everybody's hero at the time. Jack got a lot of negative press because of it. Reporters were quite cruel but he didn't let it phase him. He didn't let the press or Palmer intimidate him and just kept playing great golf.

Jack quietly went on his way and kept winning. Finally, the press began to accept him. They couldn't deny the fact that he was a great golf hero, and finally they began to write about him as a hero. But in the beginning, they had painted him as a villain. I thought the press was quite cruel about it and that was my first experience about how biased and emotional reporters can be.

I believe Jack made members of the press think a bit more deeply about how they wrote about players. Since then, I don't think they've been quite as apt to condemn and bury someone who beats their current hero.

In 1988, *Golf Magazine* honored a group of players they called golf heroes, in observance of the centennial of American golf. It was a gala evening at the Waldorf-Astoria in New York, and I was included among the honored players. I enjoyed the night more as a spectator. I can't say I was looking forward to it, because I don't enjoy such occassions, but it turned out to be an exciting evening because they managed to bring everybody together, even Ben Hogan, who rarely makes public appearances.

It was a media event, sponsored by the media, for the media. That night, it was announced that a committee had selected Jack as Golfer of the Century. You could almost predict that Jack would be selected, and if I had an extra thousand dollars to bet that night, I would have bet on Jack.

If *I* had chosen a golfer of the century, I would probably have gone with Bobby Jones. Jones was more revered than Jack. Of course, it will take a while to find out how history receives Jack.

Bobby Jones achieved so much in such a short time. He wasn't just a great player, he must have been a tremendous human being. I don't think anybody was ever as well loved as Bobby Jones was and is—not even Arnold Palmer.

MARLENE HAGGE

Marlene Hagge is one of my closest friends on the tour today. At fifty-five, she's celebrating her fortieth year on the LPGA Tour. Marlene turned professional in 1949, when she was sixteen years old, and played in the few existing pro tournaments, although the LPGA was not officially organized until 1950. So, when she tees up for the first tournament of 1990, Marlene will become the only professional athlete I've ever heard of who has played in the major leagues of any sport during *six* decades.

She is a unique individual. She looks great, takes great care of herself, and is a fine physical specimen. She still hits the ball awfully well and, physically, can play as long as she wants to. It just depends on her motivation.

Marlene was very kind to me when I first came on the tour. She's a very caring individual and usually the first one to help a rookie. Still, I was very surprised at her kindness in my first year. She was a big star, having been the leading money-winner in 1956, and was our first glamour girl. I was just a chubby kid from New Mexico. I didn't know her too well, other than knowing who she was. Marlene and her husband, Bob Hagge, lived in Florida. When the 1959 tour was coming to a close, Marlene said to me, "If you'd like to work on your game this winter and don't have a place to go, you can just come down to Florida and stay with Bob and me."

I thought that was one of the nicest things I'd ever heard and I've never forgotten it. Of course, I remind Marlene that she has always loved the underdog! We've shared a lot of good times in golf since and we've certainly maintained a very close friendship through the years.

Marlene has a lot of nice qualities and still has a lot of little girl in her. She's also emotional. Sometimes we have terrific arguments, but it's never personal. Friends laugh at us now but, one year, we served on the LPGA board together and got in an explosive argument at a meeting. I was yelling at her, she was yelling at me, but we weren't taking it personally. We were just arguing, which we both love to do.

Some of the board members told us later that they had been concerned about whether we were going to hit each other. That really surprised both of us because neither of us was really mad,

When I was inducted into the World Golf Hall of Fame, Peggy Kirk Bell, a fine player and longtime friend, did the honors.

although the other players thought we were. We still have loud debates and it's great fun. Sometimes we room together, if there's a place to stay with a kitchen. She's a wonderful cook. Marlene and I will always be great friends.

SAM SNEAD

Sam Snead and I were partners in the J.C. Penney Mixed-Team Championship in the late 1970s. Sam was a very good partner, but he played with me under a threat! It's no secret, nor do I think Sam would deny it, that he's not the easiest person in the world to get along with.

Moments of concentration over the years. The LPGA tour has been my life since 1959, and I've loved every minute of it. (*Sandpit photo by J. M. Maira*)

Joe Phillips, an executive with Wilson Sporting Goods, asked me to play with Sam in the team championship. In the past, Sam had been very hard on some of his partners although a couple had been able to play with him and do very well. Patty Berg was one. Patty just wouldn't take anything from Sam, or take any of his remarks personally. In team play, success is a matter of matching personalities.

I told Joe that I would be glad to play with Sam, but that I was not going to take anything from him and Joe had better inform Sam of that. If Sam agreed to behave, I'd play, but the minute he started riding me or making me feel uncomfortable, tell Sam that I'll quit! Life's too short. I'm not going to take any kind of abuse. Well, Joe told him and we played. During the tournament we were sitting in the players' grill and one of the men professionals said that Sam had been talking about my ultimatum in the locker room.

Sam had said, "She said she'd walk in and, boy, I gotta be on my good behavior!"

He was. We got along very well and I really enjoyed playing with him. He is such a wonderful player and I pull for him as hard as I pull for anybody.

Sam has such a wonderful golf swing; it's smooth and it always looks effortless. He has a terrific competitive spirit and is still really competitive. That's why he still plays and manages to shoot in the 70s. As a competitor, Sam gives no quarter to anyone. No mercy!

I have a great deal of respect for Sam. His record speaks for itself, and he does have a marvelous golf swing, which he learned up in the hills of West Virginia. Sam is like Byron and Ben. They were the pioneers who developed the fundamentals of the golf swing and proved the validity of the fundamentals time and time again. That's why these three players lasted so long and were so great.

Sometimes these pioneers created new techniques, just as Harry Vardon had done in the earlier days. It's funny, but there's always a "new" technique—like the square-to-square method, which was promoted years ago, or today's new fad, which is hitting from the right side—but none of these theories work unless the fundamentals are correct. Theories are great, but the fundamentals are going to see you through.

NANCY LOPEZ

Nancy Lopez had no immediate impact on our tour when she turned pro in 1976. It took her about one year, then she made an outstanding impact. She won nine tournaments in one season. It proved to doubters that one player, if she was good enough, could dominate our tour. I still say that today. If a player wants to, if she has that desire, she can dominate.

Nancy brought an awful lot to the LPGA. When she turned pro, money was a motivation, to some degree, but Nancy loves to win. That's what she's out there for. She makes no bones about it and I think that's marvelous. Why would players want to be out there, having to practice and go through some of the hardships that we encounter, and not try to be as good as they can be? I just can't understand athletes who settle for less than their best. So, I can relate to Nancy in that way. She loves to win and she hates to lose. With that attitude, money is just not enough for her. That's why she made such an impact on women's golf. She joined the tour and was ready to go. She beat all of us, beat our ears down, and I think that's just great.

When Nancy came on tour, we had a commissioner, Ray Volpe, who believed in very strong marketing. Unfortunately, Ray's way of handling Nancy was successful at first, but it backfired later. Volpe marketed Nancy quite well, but he promoted and marketed only one player. When Nancy cooled off, nobody knew any of our other players. JoAnne Carner was still playing quite well in that era, yet her name was never mentioned. The headline always said, either, ''Nancy Wins!'' or, ''Nancy Loses!''

I thought it was unfortunate that Ray used Nancy as he did. She had to make all the press appearances, which was exhausting and bad for her. She finally began saying no, because she was doing everything. Ray, also unfortunately, convinced the sponsors that, if they didn't have Nancy Lopez in their tournament, they were not going to have a successful event. It wasn't true, but Ray did a good job of convincing them. There was a lot of pressure put on Nancy and we had unhappy sponsors when she couldn't play in a tournament. Nancy handled it very well, in spite of Ray, and still handles it very well. That's a lot of responsibility on any one player's back.

Now we have good name recognition of our players. Ours is not a one-star tour. Other players who played well at that time were Patty Sheehan, Betsy King, and Beth Daniel. Very few players could have measured up to Nancy's rookie year. It was unfair to think they could, and Beth, for example, got a bad rap. Some of the press claimed that Beth wasn't so great when compared to Nancy, when, in essence, Beth was and is a great player, just not in the same way.

Such press treatment didn't help Beth and didn't help our tour, because we had a really good player in Beth. We still do. She is just now recovering from those years and beginning to get her feet back on the ground.

That was a great lesson for all of us. You cannot have a one-woman tour. Yes, Nancy was great, is great, and will be great. However, there are other great players out there. They may not have the same charisma as Nancy, but they certainly have the same playing ability.

Betsy King was a slow starter, but she will be playing for a long time. You're going to see her name a lot. Betsy will be a contender week after week.

Now that Pat Bradley is in better health, her name will be up at the top again because she's as strong as a horse. Pat is emerging. She's no flash in the pan.

Amy Alcott, I'm not sure about. I think she has to get her priorities back in line. Amy has always had a thing about what she calls, "variety and diversification!" I say this jokingly, but she has spread herself too thin and her game is suffering because of it. Amy has played well, at times, but I think she could be even better.

We have a great international contingent. Ayako Okamoto of Japan is a wonderful player. Laura Davies, an English player, is one to watch. It's really up to Laura as to how good she wants to be. She has all the athletic attributes, now it's up to her. She could be a devastating player but, if she doesn't want it enough or if it's not that important to her, then she probably won't be the great star that she could be.

Liselotte Neumann, of Sweden, is outstanding. Liselotte has a lot of pluses. She's 1988 U.S. Women's Open champion and is knocking on the door in a lot of other tournaments. Her game is getting really good and I think we'll be seeing a lot of her.

We'll be seeing more foreign players in the winner's circle on the LPGA Tour, just as we'll see more foreign players winning on the PGA Tour. I don't believe the Americans are getting weaker, I think we're drawing two or three players from each golfing nation. They are always the best and most outstanding players of their country, so they will naturally do well here. I feel that we're lucky that they want to come to the United States and play our tour.

THE FINISH

A lot of people ask me when I'm going to retire. I honestly don't know. I'm still enjoying the game and see nothing wrong with making golf a lifetime career. If you love what you're doing, why quit? In the back of my mind, I have an idea that I'll continue to compete as long as I can. I've known great players who retired, then seemed to wish that they had played longer.

I've been fortunate to have won as much as I have. Winning, of course, is so personal that you can't really explain or share that with anyone. Each win is unique.

Golf has given me a great opportunity to travel and to meet really outstanding, everyday, wonderful people. I've made some great friendships and have seen some parts of life that I might not otherwise have known. I've seen other cultures and observed how other people around the world live and react. It has been a terrific education and I don't know of another career that would have given me that. I can't think of anything that has been more exciting. Golf has meant everything to me.

Index